BOOKS BY JOHN COLLIER

Novels

FULL CIRCLE

DEFY THE FOUL FIEND

HIS MONKEY WIFE

Collections

FANCIES AND GOODNIGHTS

PRESENTING MOONSHINE

THE DEVIL AND ALL

THE TOUCH OF NUTMEG

THE JOHN COLLIER READER

PARADISE LOST

Milton's
PARADISE LOST

Screenplay for Cinema of the Mind by
John Collier

Alfred A. Knopf New York 1973

Wood engravings by Carol Iselin

This is a Borzoi Book published by Alfred A. Knopf, Inc.
Copyright © 1973 by John Collier
All rights reserved under International and Pan-American Copyright Conventions.
Published in the United States by Alfred A. Knopf, Inc., New York,
and simultaneously in Canada by Random House of Canada Limited, Toronto.
Distributed by Random House, Inc., New York.

Library of Congress Cataloging in Publication Data
Collier, John (date)   Milton's Paradise lost.
I. Milton, John, 1608–1674. Paradise lost.
I. Title.
PR6005.036M5   822'.9'12   72-171153
ISBN 0-394-47311-6
ISBN 0-394-70964-0 (pbk)

Manufactured in the United States of America
First Edition

WHATEVER IS MINE IN THESE PAGES
AND PARTICULARLY IN THE PORTRAYAL OF EVE
IS RESPECTFULLY DEDICATED TO

H. H. C.

THE APOLOGY

It was entirely without trepidation that I embarked upon this act of pillage. My first objective was the making of a screenplay out of the most dramatic, spectacular and significant parts of Milton's epic, much as certain Romans built their lesser dwellings of materials quarried from the palaces and the monuments of a grander past. Or as the butcher hews his steaks and his sirloins from the unresisting carcass of even the lordliest of bulls. Or, the pious may say, as the hyena . . .

The truth is, a screenwriter of my sort pays no reverence, nor feels he owes any, to even the most august original. All his duty is to what he hopes, always in vain, will appear on the screen.

Printing such a piece of work, even modified as this is, is a more ticklish proposition. Print, after all, is the medium of the epic itself. One might be accused of chewing great poetry into some sort of insipid mash for the benefit of the digest reader. Or, worse yet, of an upstart attempt to edge up to Milton on his own ground, and, taking hold of his cloak, unnoticed by him, endeavouring to pass oneself off as some sort of relation, however distant and however poor. Either prospect might well cause the boldest to hesitate, and make the wise refrain. Having no such end in view, I did neither.

My first purpose in writing this version was to preserve certain aspects of the screenplay, with which, such is the affectionate nature of my kind, I was in love. In particular, I wanted to retain the pace and immediacy of a certain energetic roughness, which is something quite apart from poetic or literary values.

This thing here is a parade of scenes based on Milton's glorious and appalling images, peopled with hideous or radiant monsters, and with archetypes of human beings caught in the pregnant situations of the fable.

Many of Milton's jewels are rough at the edges in this version, having been rudely ripped from their rich setting. I like them rough at the edges.

I have never hesitated to use a cliché in place of the poet's lofty and luminous language when, as sometimes strangely happened, the change seemed to impart enough crude energy to bring up an image clearer and more vivid into the mind's eye.

The ideas in *Paradise Lost* arise out of profound scholarship, but they are not profound in themselves, being a magnificent but quite orthodox expression of the religious beliefs of three hundred years ago. I do not share these beliefs, and I have substituted other ideas, also not profound in themselves, but which are more in accord with those commonly held today.

Some major portions of the poem have been entirely omitted. Some recount past events sufficiently conveyed in the opening scenes. Others are set in Heaven. Heaven might be adequately expressed in music and even to some extent in words, if they are Milton's words. Unfortunately any attempt to conjure up a definite picture results in something more fit for the calendar than for eternity. I have left out yet other passages because they call for the representation of God in person, which would make for a very embarrassing performance.

Certain great scenes have been worn thin by time, and some others are beautifully illuminated by knowledge that was not available when the original was written. Speech is such a different thing in the dramatic form that almost none of Milton's verse dialogue can be adjusted to it, except for some tremendous lines in the first two books of the poem, which have a quality of their own.

These books contain the basic premise of the dramatic story and all the first great movement of the action. The speeches, at their peak, are the product of the most urgent necessity and the most intense passion acting on a great intelligence. I have been able to take some of these peak lines and, cropping and curbing them as far as my strength allowed, I have used their sense and force and feeling to drive the action on.

Even such jagged fragments echo with enough of the original resonance and rhythm to arouse the question of how they will fall upon a modern ear. It seems to me that, as long as they are spoken plainly and without any added expressiveness, they will sound exactly as they should.

In the later books the speeches become less simple and direct. Others have guessed at an ambivalence on the part of the poet toward certain characters, or values or issues. It is a matter on which I am neither qualified nor inclined to pronounce. Whatever the cause, I have found that after the stupendous council of war in the second of the twelve books it was necessary to use such words as I could muster for myself, which of course means weaker words. Perhaps this is not entirely a disadvantage when Adam and Eve enter the scene. Being human, it seems only fitting that they should speak with less than the tongues of archangels.

In the first two books of *Paradise Lost* the defeated rebels fall from

Heaven *with hideous ruin and combustion down* into the burning lake. Satan extricates himself, and raises and rallies his followers. They erect a temple-palace-fortress to be called Pandemonium. In its shelter grand strategy is discussed, a counterattack decided on, and its objective chosen—God's new creation, Man. Satan himself will reconnoitre. The horrid continents of Hell are over-flown, Sin and Death confronted at Hell gate, Satan flies through the universe in search of the new-made Earth, and finds it.

Who would, or could, steer aside from such a cataract of action? The speeches, as if to make themselves heard above the torrent, seem as they reach their crest to shout from the printed page. They throb with an urgency that bursts out of all rounded eloquence and into an utterance as natural to this century as to their own. Churchill's growl of defiance after Dunkirk was not essentially more modern in tone than the undaunted speech with which Satan maintains his resolution after the fall—

> *What though the field be lost?*
> *All is not lost—the unconquerable will,*
> *And study of revenge, immortal hate,*
> *And courage never to submit or yield.*

In the epic, it's true, Satan speaks these words only to Beelzebub, while both still lie prone in the molten lava. In a dramatic version, with the scene more present to the eye, such ordered thought would imply indifference to the fire. And, if the hosts of the fallen are also to be seen, this all-important speech, the whole spirit of the resistance, should be audible to them as well. Therefore I have reserved it until Satan can deliver it from the shore, and his words burst like rockets over the seething, struggling crowd, and it is possible to show their utterance and their impact almost simultaneously, and thus convey their magical effect on the morale of the defeated legions.

Now we have a new element for consideration. Satan and all his followers are doomed to *torture without end*.

> *A dungeon horrible, on all sides round,*
> *As one great furnace flamed, yet from those flames*
> *No light, but rather darkness visible*
> *Served only to discover sights of woe,*
> *Regions of sorrow, doleful shades, where peace*
> *And rest can never dwell, hope never comes*
> *That comes to all, but torture without end*
> *Still urges, and a fiery deluge, fed*
> *With ever-burning sulphur unconsumed.*
> *Such place Eternal Justice had prepared*
> *For those rebellious, here their prison ordained*
> *In utter darkness. . . .*

Yet Satan's shout brings them crowding to the shore, healed of the worst effects of the Hellish fire; soon ranked in martial order, and with music, banners and dazzling arms.

Moreover, they now proceed to raise a superb structure, more magnificent than all the temples and palaces in which Babylon and Egypt enshrined their gods or enthroned their kings.

Milton explains this extraordinary change in the circumstances of those condemned to *torture without end* plainly enough but not very simply. Satan, he says, lay—

> *Chained on the burning lake; nor ever thence*
> *Had risen or heaved his head but that the will*
> *And high permission of all-ruling Heaven*
> *Left him at large to his own dark designs,*
> *That with reiterated crimes he might*
> *Heap on himself damnation, while he sought*
> *Evil to others, and enraged might see*
> *How all his malice served but to bring forth*
> *Infinite goodness, grace, and mercy, shown*
> *On Man by him seduced, but on himself*
> *Treble confusion, wrath, and vengeance poured.*

In other words, the prisoner was paroled in order that he might commit fresh crimes and incur a yet heavier sentence. Man, at the cost of death to all and damnation to many, was to serve as bait in this outrageous trap.

Luckily Milton, after setting down this explanation, shows us, without naming it, a more likely and a more tolerable one. He shows us the effects of a force that originated in Hell and that has been used on earth, in Heaven's despite, throughout the ages. Frazer could have named it; it is magic. See how Pandemonium, that fairy palace, rose out of the sulphurous, burned-out soil! *It rose like an exhalation, with the sound of dulcet symphonies and voices sweet.* What better demonstration could we have of the operation of the magic power? And what better formula than Satan's other great dictum, more profound than the first:

> *The mind is its own place, and in itself*
> *Can make a Heaven of Hell, a Hell of Heaven.*

Consider also that Satan's companions are destined to appear on earth as the false gods of the heathen, and Satan himself as the horned and hoofed deity of the most antique and the most persistent of all idolatries, and later as the dark presence at black mass and witch's sabbath, whose broomstick devotees, fumbling with the last rags and tatters of the ancient mystery, have been pursued by the Church with fire and torment after the great example shown here at the beginning.

Which brings us to the opening of the third book, and into the presence of God, an encounter I had looked forward to with well-founded apprehension.

God sees Satan flying toward the world. (I have taken his wings off, by the way, as boys are said to do with flies; a disgusting practice, but not as disgusting as ever-burning sulphur unconsumed, or the stake and faggots, or the ovens, or the atom bomb, or fire bombing, or napalm, or as any of the detestable wretches who have made use of such abominations.)

God sees Satan, and He foresees that *Man will hearken to his glozing lies and easily transgress.*

It would seem a simple matter to caution the prospective victim. Sure enough, God sends a warning to Adam, though not, please note, to Eve. Presumably He must also have foreseen the fact that Satan's lies would be told to Eve, and that it was Eve who would be deceived by them, and that she would be the first to eat of the fruit. Nevertheless, it is to Adam the warning is sent, not only because God takes no cognisance of the female, but also for a more extraordinary reason: knowing that Adam will fall, God does not wish him to have any excuse. The Archangel Raphael is sent to put him on the alert *lest he pretend surprisal, unadmonished, unforewarned.* Infinite goodness, grace, and mercy!

The ill-disposed may well ask why God was so insistent that Adam should not acquire the knowledge of good and evil. Could it be that, given and ability to recognise evil when he saw it, Man might come to an embarrassing conclusion as to which side had triumphed in the primal conflict? Possibly there is some other resolution of the monstrous inconsistency between infinite goodness and unbounded vindictiveness, but, not finding it in *Paradise Lost,* I hastily backed away into a thicket of lesser contradictions, where I found myself quite comfortably at home.

The first and most important contradiction of all allowed me to avert my gaze from unworthy motives and dreadful deeds, and to accord the Deity the divinest of all his attributes—perfection. Perfection imprisons its possessor as in a crystal; the least move, to better or worse or merely to other, and there is a shattering. With one or two minor exceptions this sublime immobility is in line with the epic, in which, having done His worst at the very outset, God abstains from present and positive action, which is all that this dramatised version makes use of. He therefore remains, as gloriously as you please, off stage.

Not so Satan. His unremitting enterprise and ever-changing moods command attention at every step. It is often asserted, though not by the author himself, that Satan is the true hero of *Paradise Lost.*

Certainly no figure in history or in myth was ever adorned with such a panoply of heroic virtues. Resplendent in aspect, *nor less than Archangel ruined*—and even ruined is a romantic addition to an archangel!—of dauntless courage, *who durst defy the Omnipotent in arms,* steadfast in the bitterest adversity, ingenious in escape, subtle and eloquent, he retains the love and devotion of all the millions who have followed him into unspeakable disaster. His situation is in itself heroic: he is the rebel against the Establishment, the defeated, the exile, the endungeoned, the resurgent, and the guerrilla. To cap it all, he is traduced. He is never referred to except in such terms as evil, proud, cruel, and the like, but we watch in vain for some example of his wickedness.

It will be observed, however, that all the iniquities of which Satan is accused are manifested severally by his closest associates. Mammon, Moloch, Belial and the rest are each the embodiment of a different deadly sin. It has appeared to me not unjust to suggest at times that these individual personalities might have another existence as parts of Satan's own nature. Or, shifting the focus again, it seems possible to present God and Satan as two of the great opposites that contest the universe: the *status quo* and change, the Establishment and the radical; matter and anti-matter; in this case, good and evil.

According to such a fancy Satan at times may comprehend not only his followers but Hell itself (which Milton says he carries always in his heart). Or, to reduce the greatest of things to the infinitesimal, God in his static perfection might be likened to a crystal, and Satan to the virus which rebels, invades, corrupts and evolves.

Considered as an individual, and as described by Milton, Satan seems to have done nothing worse than do the general run of heroes. He has rebelled and he has attempted, with a measure of success, to subvert his Adversary's creatures. These, surely, are acts of war rather than war crimes, to make a nice distinction. He inflicts no tortures. To the contrary, he is moved to tears, *tears such as Angels weep,* by the condition of his lowliest followers after the tortures inflicted on them by Another.

Nevertheless, though heroic in the extreme, Satan is not the hero of this particular story. For one thing, his objective, though close to the core of the matter, is not at its very heart, and it is essentially negative. For another, Satan is not human. It would seem that heroism must be encased in our littleness, if only to burst out of it.

Adam, of course, is human by definition. It is true he lacks those little weaknesses we recognise as implicit in the term. Such weaknesses may not be as endearing as their possessors fondly believe; on the other hand, their conspicuous absence is not altogether attractive.

Milton decorates Adam with the names of innumerable fine qualities, but these, like the pejoratives applied to Satan, lack enactment. Thus they remain only words, as formal and unmoving as the measured compliments with which Adam himself prefaces his addresses to Eve.

It must be admitted that Adam, hitherto no more than a prize specimen, suddenly and rather incredibly has his great, romantic moment, a moment of heroism even, in view of the dreadful penalty involved, when he throws in his lot with Eve rather than repudiate his love and remain in favour and immortal in Paradise. Alas, immediately afterward, in the brief space between his utterance of the high resolve and implementing it by eating the fruit, he manages to qualify his sacrifice by persuading himself that the threatened punishment will not be rigorously applied.

Even apart from this, Adam has appeared as such a paragon of all the deadlier virtues that his sudden flare of heroism seems strangely pale and unreal, like a flame in daylight, lacking its dark opposite to show it for what it is. Someone less unrelievedly serene and noble, even someone weak, timid, and uncertain, might at once surprise and convince us by a breathless act of daring and thus emerge as the true hero of the story.

And finally, the true hero of any story is surely the one who does the essential thing, the deed which is that story's *raison d'être*. *Paradise Lost* is the story of the loss of Paradise and the attainment of the knowledge of good and evil—and the character who loses the one and gains for us the other is Eve.

For this reason, I have ventured to add a little, here and there, to Eve's personality as depicted by Milton. I have tried to endow her with a stirring of instincts that the bliss of Paradise itself cannot wholly satisfy, and with a little sympathy for greatness and beauty cast down, and with a flicker of vision on such matters as the close relationship between love and sin, and between death and new life. If these slight changes, and the darker tinge I have infused into her complexion, make this Eve seem an unwarrantable distortion of Milton's concept, I shall have failed; if in spite of this the reader still finds her lovable, the attempt will not have been entirely in vain.

J.C.

P.S. I have, in three separate places, used single lines from Shakespeare, Blake, and Gerard Manley Hopkins. I would not have stolen them except that my need was great.

PARADISE LOST

THE BLUE NIGHT OF INFINITE SPACE
We are moving upward into a region where the blue is lighter and clearer.

A SINGLE STAR
It becomes visible high up and far away. It grows larger, more liquid, a golden drop. Soon it assumes a form like that of a comet, its head uppermost, its lengthening tail streaming downward.

Two rays of light diverge horizontally from the comet's head.

We hear sounds so deep we scarcely recognise them as sounds. It could be the regular thudding, more felt than heard, of the heartbeat of some enormous animal.

Waves of light pulse through the blue around us. The whole endless void is quaking. It might be a tank of highly explosive liquid becoming mysteriously agitated as it approaches flash-point.

The golden star is still increasing in size. Now we see the most minute, yet diamond-bright, points of light winking here and there on the surface of the tail that streams down from it. These bright flashes appear at the same intervals as those between the sounds, and between the pulsations of light in the blue.

We are accelerating our approach to the star. The horizontal rays spread wider and wider on each side. We sweep upward at tremendous speed, and then more slowly as we approach a point on the ray which extends to our right. This point is far from, and soon out of sight of, the streaming tail of the comet.

THE RAMPARTS OF HEAVEN

What seemed like a ray of light is an endless line of precipices rising from an unseen base in the deeps of space and extending as far as the eye can see. The face of the precipice is of the whitish-gold colour of some auriferous rock. Along the top of the cliff, huge blocks of this rock, roughly hewn, are built into battlements.

HEAVEN

For a moment the sweep of our flight carries us a little above the level of the ramparts. Somewhere in the radiant, blue-gold haze in the region behind the battlements, we catch a vague glimpse of towers and palaces, more or less like those imagined in a golden cloud at sunset.

BELOW THE RAMPARTS

The curve of our flight takes us down again so that the edge of the ramparts cuts off any further view of the interior of Heaven. We are now sweeping along at great speed on an arc which descends very slowly. We are headed in the direction of what appeared to us as the tail of the comet.

The flashes of light are becoming more and more vivid, and the dull, thudding sound becomes louder and sharper.

THE FALLING TORRENT

Now we see the tail again, at a great distance ahead of us. It looks like a broad, golden river flowing over the ramparts and plunging out of sight into the gulf below.

The sound of deafening explosions. Blinding flashes of light. The surface of this waterfall is being violently bombarded with bolts which burst into newborn suns.

LOOKING UPWARD

The curve of our flight is taking us down beside the torrent as it falls into the abyss. But, looking upward, we can see clusters of the newborn suns as they stream away into the deep sapphire of the firmament, taking on the forms of constellations familiar to us. We recognize the Great Bear, Orion, the Pleiades, Aquarius . . .

THE NIAGARA OF FALLING ANGELS

Nearer and louder explosions draw our eyes to the golden torrent ahead of us. It now has a finely rippled aspect, as if it might be made up of millions of newly hatched fish.

Between the explosions, we hear another sound—the sound of the fall. The rush of a hundred million falling bodies combines with countless shouts of rage and screams of pain to blend into a sound such as we have never heard before.

The explosions are causing fierce fires to break out on the surface—miles wide—of this falling substance. One, erupting on the edge nearest to us, sends up great spouts of the stuff.

THE DRIFTING SPRAY

Sprays and mists of the cascading liquid float out to meet us. They coalesce into a cloud. We enter the ragged, vapourous fringes of the cloud.

THE BUBBLES

The mist is made up of tiny droplets like miniature bubbles. These bubbles swirl around us. One of them, as if coming from nowhere, sweeps by startlingly close.

A BUBBLE

It is made of six or eight living creatures. These are gigantic and glorious beings with beautiful, stricken faces and flying hair. They wear minimal golden armour, such as we are accustomed to associate with demigods or angels.

Other bubbles are passing close to us.

OTHER BUBBLES

Some of them are disorganised. The angels spinning around in them have been mutilated by the explosion. These bubbles are flying apart. The broken creatures which compose them spin out individually.

Now we fly clear of the cloud.

THE DRIFTING SPRAY

The torrent itself is plunging down at a fantastic speed. The misty spray is scudding swiftly past us as if driven by the force of the explosions or by the whirlwind fire storms on the surface of the waterfall.

THE FALL

Seeing it alternately as a whole and in detail, we realise that the bubbles, the spray, and the torrent are all of the same substance—live angels the molecules of it.

THE TORRENT AND THE RAMPARTS

We see clearly the wide expanse of the golden waterfall, its surface sullied by hideous fires crackling and reddening and smoking all over it. The waterfall falls away from the ramparts of Heaven, and drops like a golden band, vertically, into the abyss.

THE FINAL BOMBARDMENT

We swoop down toward the surface of the torrent. A brief but violent stepping up of the explosions finally disintegrates the cataract of doomed angels. The whole fall is atomised. All space seems to be filled, as with big flakes of snow, with myriads of these falling creatures. Some mutilated, some in flames, they spread far and wide in a thick downpour, with now and then a single agonized face or a broken body sweeping past so close as almost to touch us.

THE GOLDEN SNOWFALL, FLUSHED WITH FIRE, BLACKENS

The myriads of the damned begin to char in mid-space.

As they blacken, the light changes. The blue is infused with a ruby glow spreading upward. A bar of vivid red becomes visible below. It grows longer and wider. A sound of furious crackling and hissing rises from its surface. It is a lake of fire, spreading as far as the eye can see, and the angels are falling thickly into it.

THE LAKE OF FIRE

Its depth is such as to come just short of covering the prostrate, writhing figures which are now thickly packed in it, and which spread out beyond the limits of visibility.

The outcry of the damned, which was subdued to a muted grieving over the soft snowfall in the previous scene, now becomes more intense and hideous than before.

A GROUP OF THE DAMNED

A dozen or twenty individuals almost submerged, writhing, screaming. Bubbles rise from a sunken head, each bursting into a fragment of a scream of agony. Burning faces raise themselves above the molten lava for just long enough to eject shrieks like missiles.

SATAN

One of these figures, heaving and plunging like the rest, has more purpose in his convulsive movements. He rears up his terrible, blackened, noseless, lipless, tongueless, eyeless, smouldering head, but he utters no sound. He keeps his hands from automatically lifting themselves clear of the lava. He presses down on them long enough to draw up a knee under him. He is trying to rise to his burned-off feet. He pitches forward again, splashing up the lava. He is burned to incandescence, like a log that is red all the way through, ready to fall to pieces.

Satan does not fall to pieces. His stance becomes a little more assured. He lifts his head high. He raises a hand, flaring and smoking like a torch, in a gesture of triumph, of leadership.

SATAN'S HAND

It ceases to burn. It becomes a charred claw. It is on the way to a complete healing.

SATAN

Standing erect. The lava pours from his head and shoulders, and leaks from his scanty armour. It runs in corrosive rivulets over his healing flesh, burning out new channels as it does so.

Below the surface of the shallow lake, Satan's legs, almost up to his knees, are still burning. His recovering face shows his agony, and his contempt for it.

THE FIERY LAKE. VARIOUS ANGELS. THE SHORE

A dense smoke rises from the burning angels. Visibility is very limited. Now and then a blast of searing wind blows some of the smoke aside, showing us more angels writhing and wallowing in the lava.

Looking around, Satan catches a glimpse of a low-lying shore; its surface solid but still smoking.

Satan wades through the close-packed bodies of his followers toward the shore.

SATAN

His resplendent beauty is blasted, but it is all the more appealing for that. Whatever perfection of form has been lost is compensated for by new elements born of his defeat and suffering. We shall see that courage, gentleness, sweetness, understanding, sensitivity are all raised to a level which makes him almost irresistible. Lifting his face, he inhales the sulphurous air. He feels it to be charged with a mysterious force. He is strangely exhilarated. He wrenches an exultant cry out of what perhaps began as a groan of agony.

SATAN'S FOLLOWERS BECOME AWARE OF HIM

Hearing his ringing cry, those nearest to Satan realise that their leader is close at hand, upright and active. Blind faces are raised in a desperate attempt to see him. Fingerless hands paw at his knees as he passes. The awareness of his presence and his purpose seems to spread wider and wider, like a ripple spreading over the sea of burning angels. Wherever the curtains of smoke are blown aside, we see blackened and shapeless creatures heaving themselves out of the lava and falling back again. A few of the most powerful struggle to their knees, and collapse. One or two even gain their feet and stumble forward, only to pitch face down into the hissing lava. Others, determined to see their leader, support themselves on their hands regardless of the pain, and lift out their heads and shoulders long enough for their features to be somewhat restored, and they look devotedly toward their lord. But then the agony becomes unbearable and they raise their burning hands, and at once fall forward again.

SATAN AND BEELZEBUB

Close to the shore a giant form rears itself up in Satan's path. It lifts stumps of hands toward him. It totters and is about to collapse. Satan recognises the dreadful remnants of the burned-off face. It is Beelzebub. Wise, subtle, and unscrupulous, he is, next to Satan, the greatest of the fallen angels.

Satan makes a stride forward and catches Beelzebub as he falls. His arm around him, he half drags, half carries Beelzebub to the shore.

LAKE SHORE: SATAN AND BEELZEBUB

The healing of the fallen angels is rapid and complete in proportion to the strength of these spirits, and their strength is in proportion to their rank. Beelzebub's flesh is slower than Satan's in restoring itself.

Satan is supporting Beelzebub, looking into his face, impatient to see it healed.

Satan lifts his hand as if to feel the mysterious force in the air. His fingers become charged with this force. He uncertainly passes his quivering fingers over Beelzebub's face. As he does so his lips tremble in the whisper of a word that is unfamiliar to him, potent, almost terrifying.

Satan is amazed to see that with the passage of his hand, and the utterance of the mysterious word, Beelzebub's face is instantly healed.

Satan has begun to discover magic, the force which he will later introduce on Earth, where it will develop in the form of paleolithic cave rites, and the rituals of the neolithic shaman in his horns and skins, in voodoo, in witchcraft, in black masses attended by Satan in person, and in all other evocations of the powers of darkness. Magic is to be the weapon of the resistance which Satan sets up against the power of God.

BEELZEBUB

He is looking in wonderment at his master's exultant face.

As soon as he is able to tear his eyes away, Beelzebub looks right and left at the appalling scene around him. His expression changes. He looks back at Satan despairingly.

> BEELZEBUB
> Utter defeat!

Satan points to the bubbling, crackling lava.

> SATAN
> Are we still lying there,
> Beelzebub?

> BEELZEBUB
> Your legions lie there, Satan,
> and they burn.

Satan scarcely hears. He is lifting his hand, feeling the air, engrossed by the peculiar element he detects.

> SATAN
> There's something in this air . . .

He steps back into the edge of the lava, where a hideously mutilated archangel is writhing in the shallows. Satan momentarily ignores this unfortunate. He halts, and halts Beelzebub.

> SATAN
> . . . a force. From which I
> breathe in strength. You feel it?

Beelzebub stands ankle-deep in the hissing, seething lava and says piteously:

> BEELZEBUB
> Satan, I feel the fire.

Satan spatters deeper into the lava, feeling it, despising it.

> SATAN
> *His* fire! To burn His creatures!
> But we're no longer His.

Satan addresses his final words to the fallen archangel, as he begins to lift him.

SATAN

So burn no more!

The archangel, supported by Satan, totters toward the shore. A lesser angel, hitherto unnoticed, hugs the archangel's leg with two remnants of arms, and is dragged along with him.

BEELZEBUB

He regains courage and forces himself into the lava to haul another angel out of it.

SATAN

He wades deeper, and rescues another, to whom another clings, and to him yet another.

Clusters and chains of victims are pulled out of the hissing lava. A magnetic current seems to flow from Satan through the others, even at three or four removes, so that some submerged creature, merely by touching with his fingerless hands, is able to hold on.

Through the shifting smoke we see certain giant figures, stronger than the rest, getting to their feet, tottering, falling, getting up again. These are archangels of the highest rank, some of them close aides of Satan. He sees them struggling toward the shore, and shouts to them, or waves an arm. Even the gesture seems to draw them.

All this time, Satan is shouting—first to one angel and then to others:

SATAN

Up with you! Out of it!
This way! To me! Help him,
there! Lift him! Together now!
Look where Mammon stands!
Mammon, this way!

LAKE SHORE AND LAKE

On the shore, an increasing group of angels, crippled and burned but gradually recovering. Some are sprawling on the hot ground; others are squatting, sitting, or holding on to each other as they stand, like the survivors of an atomic blast.

Satan strides among them, exultant, stamping on the reeking rock. Other great archangels stumble to join him. Soon Satan, the Antichrist, is surrounded by twelve disciples or aides. These, who are destined to become twelve false gods worshipped by fallen mankind, are at once distinct individuals, and parts of Satan's mind and nature. In the latter aspect they are frequently in conflict with each other.

SATAN GREETS ASTORETH AND THAMMUZ

> SATAN
>
> Astoreth! Thammuz! Here at least we are free!
>
> ASTORETH
>
> Free?
>
> THAMMUZ
>
> In this dungeon?
>
> SATAN
>
> Where we may reign secure. For my choice, Astoreth, better to reign in Hell than serve in Heaven.
>
> BEELZEBUB
>
> And those who serve—who serve even you—in Hell?

He gestures toward:

THE LAKE

The smoke is blown aside sufficiently to show us that the small group on shore is as nothing compared with the myriads still hopelessly struggling in the lava.

SATAN STANDS ON A SLIGHT RISE

Beelzebub and Mammon motion the recovering angels and archangels to form a semicircle facing Satan, their backs to the lake. Other angels are still extricating themselves from the lava, and come dragging themselves, crawling, hobbling up to join the rear of the crowd.

Satan looks at the archangels in the front rank. Each great prince or general looks back at him sombrely. As soon as his glance releases theirs, their defeated eyes seek the ground again.

Satan first speaks to this inner circle, and in a tone at once resonant and low, at once reasoning and pleading.

> SATAN
>
> The battle is fought—and lost.

They look even more hopeless and defeated.

> SATAN
>
> *All* is not lost.

SATAN'S ARMIES

Satan now realises that he must address and inspire not only the semicircle immediately confronting him, but also all the rest of the thousand demigods and the hundred million lesser angels who are still struggling in the burning lava.

With the merest movement of his hands, as if sketching the parting of curtains, he sees through the semicircle in front of him and out across the burning lake. He rears his head high; he lifts himself to see farther; his stature increases. Now, apart from those areas hidden at times by the drifting smoke, Satan commands the whole immense scene. He cries out, loud as a trumpet:

> SATAN
>
> What though the fight be lost?

The firmament of Hell is a dome of rock many miles high. It is obscured at present by the smoke which hangs above like a brooding, metallic, lurid sky. But the rock provides an echo like a roll of thunder. Satan's voice is immensely amplified. We hear the word *what* reverberate in many repetitions. Then the word *lost* booms as if in a sound chamber, clanging like a dungeon door. Satan has to pause to allow these echoes to die down at the end of each phrase.

SATAN'S AIDES

A quick glance at them while the last word is still reverberating. They feel the first faint stirrings of renewed courage and strength.

> SATAN
>
> All is not lost.

He pauses again. The words *all* and *lost* roll to and fro across the burning sea—words of doom to the myriads who are too far off to be inspired by Satan.

AN ARCHANGEL

Standing near the beach, ankle-deep in the lava. He has only just raised himself and his features are still blackened and fuming. Hearing the two dread words rolling in the sky, the archangel, with hanging head, echoes them out of his half-obliterated mouth.

>   ARCHANGEL
>   All . . . lost . . .

OTHER ARCHANGELS

Standing, swaying, or just lifting themselves above the surface. One after another they hopelessly mumble the two words.

SATAN

More forcefully than before, he shouts:

>   SATAN
>   All is *not* lost.
>   The unconquerable will . . .

BEELZEBUB

He lifts his head and folds his arms with an air of renewed resolution.

>   SATAN
>   And study of revenge . . .

MOLOCH

Far out on the fiery lake, a singularly powerful and warlike archangel is raising himself from the lava. We shall learn that this is Moloch, who, as commander in chief of Satan's armies, ranks next after Beelzebub. Hearing the word *revenge* reverberating in the sky, he raises his fist exultingly and tears himself completely out of the clinging lava, rising to his own height in the air, and then skimming low over the surface of the lake, trailing smoke like a stricken war plane. (None of the angels has wings.) Moloch lands, restored to his full martial beauty, among the other archangels on the beach.

>   SATAN
>   Immortal hate . . .

BELIAL

Another archangel is inspired by the word *hate* to rise from the lava and fly in as Moloch did. He lands in the front rank. We shall later know him as Belial.

THE LAKE

Satan's speech, prolonged by pauses and echoes, fills thousands of spirits with the wildest excitement. They struggle to extricate themselves with the desperate agitation of flies on flypaper. Only a few succeed.

The echoes are beginning to be overlaid by the voices of angels—sometimes single angels, sometimes hundreds clamouring in chorus. Each angel, or each group, is repeating whatever phrase of Satan's most inspires them: *The unconquerable will! Study of revenge! Immortal hate!*

SATAN

Satan now raises his voice to its utmost pitch.

> SATAN
>
> . . . and courage never to submit nor yield.

PANORAMIC SHOT: LAKE AND SHORE

The excitement is wilder than ever. Echoes and voices blend in repeating Satan's last speech—sometimes in a multitudinous mumble, sometimes in massed chorus, sometimes in a single voice speaking sharply and clearly. But all the time these cries and choruses are building up to a magic incantation. Many angels extricate themselves, stumbling to the shore. The greater part fail in spite of their frantic efforts.

SATAN

> SATAN
>
> Rise now! Save yourselves!
> Or burn—forever fallen!

He raises his arms high and shouts a word in the unknown tongue, a word that booms like a gong.

THE LAKE

At this word all the myriads of angels tear themselves out of the lava. Losing the bulk of their bodies, the lake level sinks almost to insignificance. Since the flesh of the angels is no longer burning in the lava, the great clouds of smoke begin to thin out and drift away. The angels, streaming toward the shore, at first fly only a few feet above the surface. But as they crowd in toward the beach, the later arrivals are forced to come in at higher levels, so that the whole air is full of them, many of them still charred.

As this *pitchy cloud of locusts* descends on the vast level of the lake shore, it distils itself into the rank and file of a well-disciplined army on parade.

We see battalions, then companies, then platoons clustered like ants close to where Satan is standing. We see his gigantic foot behind one of the groups.

ONE OR TWO PLATOONS

These are the youngest and the weakest, and therefore the lowliest privates. They will recover less completely than their seniors. In both Heaven and Hell, rank, power, and maturity are all associated. The privates have the look of boys in their teens; their corporals and sergeants might be in their early twenties. The fair ladies' faces of these low-ranking angels are beautiful from a slight distance, but seen closer they have a blasted and withered look such as we see in people who have had skin grafts after being badly burned.

Satan's voice rolls and crashes like thunder from high above. It evokes shouts and cheers and the brandishing of weapons.

> SATAN
>
> Immortal spirits, never to be
> destroyed! Undying courage and
> undying rage! Add these, and all
> our pains shall be revenged.
> Face endless miseries! Seek
> eternal war! Strive to be thorns
> in His flesh for ever! Prepare
> yourselves! I come among you now.

On the last words, Satan is standing among the young angels. Moloch, Beelzebub, and others of his chiefs of staff almost instantaneously join him.

SATAN REVIEWS HIS TROOPS

> SATAN
>
> Well, young ones, who love me;
> whom I love so well . . .

He smiles benignly as these, unable to control their enthusiasm, break rank and come crowding around him. Some lift their hands as if to touch him, but do not quite dare to do so.

> SATAN
>
> Bruised, but not beaten—yes?

SATAN AND THE YOUNG ANGELS

Satan's smile fades as he sees, close to, the ruin of these young faces which looked so beautiful while they were still standing in line. He sees their scorched and battered armour, but most of all the tragedy in the attempted smiles with which they try to express their forgiveness, their adoration.

Satan sets his hands on the shoulders of one of these and looks closely at his withered face, and deep into his faded eyes. The sight horrifies him. He tries to speak.

SATAN

You . . . shall . . .

He stops, choked. Tears roll down his cheeks. After a second attempt, and more tears, he forces the words out.

SATAN

You shall be whole again.

Satan speaks to a wider circle. His words come brokenly.

SATAN

All of you! My brave . . . and my beloved . . . every one.

Satan's speech continues as he addresses a wide spread of his battalions.

SATAN

You shall be restored. Either by the force we find here, or by that power which He's abused. And which we'll take from Him as we reconquer Heaven.

Shouts and cheering, and brandishing of weapons.

SATAN

Meanwhile, we huddle on this reeking desert, under that hateful Eye. No more! We'll make ourselves a dwelling and a stronghold. There's power here—*now*—for that. The *Magic* power, that's in the air of Hell.

His eye travels over the sea of faces, seeking one.

SATAN

Mulciber's with us—yes?
Where's Mulciber?

Everywhere, shouts of *Mulciber!* Suddenly we notice an eddy in the crowd. Someone is being thrust forward.

Mulciber is ejected from the crowd on to the little space in front of Satan, who greets him with flattering attention.

SATAN AND MULCIBER

> SATAN
>
> Mulciber! Heaven's architect!
>
> MULCIBER
>
> God's obedient builder, rather!
>
> SATAN
>
> Builder of countless glories.
>
> MULCIBER
>
> All exactly the same. Satan,
> mine is an art. I want to create.
>
> SATAN
>
> Up there, my friend, there's
> only One who creates. One who
> rules. One who does everything,
> *is* everything.
>
> MULCIBER
>
> That's why I'm with you, Satan.
> The chance to make new things!
>
> SATAN
>
> New things indeed! But,
> Heaven's mines and
> quarries lost, of what to
> make them?
>
> MULCIBER
>
> My thoughts. My heart. My brain.
>
> SATAN
>
> Be it so, Mulciber! Build us
> here a palace and a fortress. A
> home and hive for demons, which,

> while we live in His will, we must become. *Pandemonium*, call it.
>
> MULCIBER
>
> Where, though?

He looks around. The architect is disdainful of the site. Satan points to the ground at Mulciber's feet.

> SATAN
>
> Here.
>
> MULCIBER
>
> In *this* place?
>
> SATAN
>
> The mind is its own place, and in itself can make a Heaven of Hell, a Hell of Heaven.

MULCIBER

He stands transfixed, pierced through the mind by this thought. He murmurs:

> MULCIBER
>
> The mind is its *own* place.

He is staring down at the little patch of smoky, rough, hot, granular ground immediately in front of him—the equivalent of a square yard or so. Over his shoulder we see this little patch becoming smoother, beginning to spread wider. The lines of a foundation plan are marked out on it, and grow with it as it spreads.

BEELZEBUB AND MAMMON

Beelzebub turns to Mammon, speaking quietly but with keen intellectual relish.

> BEELZEBUB
>
> The mind is its own place!

ASTORETH AND THAMMUZ

Destined to become Ishtar and Thammuz, these two represent the twin poles of sexuality. Astoreth is the feminine principle. Flushed, amorous, and depraved, he/she leans toward Thammuz and whispers:

ASTORETH

And in itself, Thammuz, can make a Heaven of Hell!

As Thammuz smiles assent, we pass on to:

MOLOCH

Standing alone, dedicated to implacable ferocity. Moloch is doomed to degenerate into that monstrous iron idol with jagged teeth and a furnace in his belly, in which the children of Tophet and of Carthage were burned alive. Later, he may be reincarnated under names even more familiar to us. He now mutters the phrase which best accords with his mood.

MOLOCH

A Hell of Heaven!

THE HOST OF THE DAMNED

Everyone finds something to excite him in Satan's threefold proposition. It runs through the crowd like fire through a stubble field. Everywhere angels are turning to one another to repeat a chosen phrase, or any combination of phrases, in tones of wonder, relief, delight, and triumph. Soon we lose the distinct words, and recognize only the sound of each phrase, repeated like bells and echoes, here chiming in musical chorus, in other places rolling over wide areas of the endless crowd.

The sounds are building up into an incantation, generating Mana, the elemental force of magic.

HIGH IN THE AIR

The fallen angels are not all upon the ground. Great squares of them, numbering a hundred or more in each direction, are standing at all levels in the air, shouting each different phrase in choral unison.

SATAN

His arms upraised, he is gathering in the immense magic force which is being generated. Becoming filled with it, he bends over to project it upon Mulciber.

MULCIBER

Mulciber, under Satan's demanding and inspiring eye, ponders the area of smooth and level soil which is spreading wider and wider in front of him.

He bends over it, crouches over it. He goes down on one hand and one knee to brood upon it more pregnantly. As it expands, Mulciber also expands.

The stuff of his body becomes more and more attenuated; it becomes semi-transparent.

There is a sort of ferment within Mulciber. As the sound of the incantation continues in strophe and antistrophe, we begin to see whole companies of tiny beings toiling in orderly gangs inside Mulciber's transparent body. They are honeycombing the soil with mines and quarries, hauling enormous blocks of stone up ramps, and raising spidery scaffoldings.

The indistinct, melodious, bell-like, echolike reiteration of the magic phrases builds up and up with ever-increasing power.

The palace is rising like music out of the ground. It is rising into Mulciber. As he bends low to draw on the ground with far-reaching finger, his arm remains fixed and resting on the ground. The columns and arches of a curving colonnade sprout up into it, replacing the substance of the arm.

At the same time we see the fragmentary outlines of a vast and complex building, made up of visions of all the palaces and citadels and prisons that ever existed. This giant complex is rising inside the torso of Mulciber, which has now drooped forward on to the ground.

MULCIBER'S HEAD

He is still trying to hold it up. His forehead and his skull have become distended, round and bare. Within them we can see the ancient symbols of masonry—the trowel, the hammer, the compass and the plumb line—flashing in and out of existence.

The indistinct chant rises to its highest pitch, and suddenly ceases. Satan's voice gathers up the words underlying the sound of the chant, and reconstitutes them in a distinct and final utterance:

> SATAN
>
> The mind is its own place, and
> in itself can make a Heaven of
> Hell, a Hell of Heaven.

On the last word, Mulciber dies. The architect has become his own building. Huge pillars have been rearing up through his cheeks. His brows, knitted in intense concentration, have been transmuted into a frowning pediment. His forehead has soared up into a dome. His mouth drops open as he dies; his chin touches the earth and is at once transformed into a grand exterior staircase. The mouth itself becomes a monumental doorway.

IN A DIFFERENT DIMENSION

> *Straight the doors,*
> *Opening their brazen folds, discover, wide*
> *Within, her ample spaces o'er the smooth*
> *And level pavement: from the archèd roof,*
> *Pendent by subtle magic, many a row*
> *Of starry lamps and blazing cressets, fed*
> *With naptha and asphaltus, yielded light*
> *As from a sky.*

Satan and his peers are standing at the head of the staircase, on the wide, flagged terrace in front of the giant doors. The doors open, revealing an endless, fragmented, dreamlike interior.

Satan strides forward into this palace, followed closely by his twelve highest officers, and at a wider interval by an indeterminate number of the great lords of Hell, the thousand demigods who comprise the grand council.

PANDEMONIUM

Vestibules, entrance halls, the great hall, glimpses of lesser halls and galleries, all fragmentary, some superimposed on others.

Satan and his entourage cross the great hall and enter a principal gallery.

THE LONG GALLERY

Its lamp-lit perspective diminishes to a black pinpoint at some unbelievable distance.

THE OUTER DOORWAY

The myriads of lower-ranking angels have kept respectfully back until their lord has passed across the main hall. Now they surge in. They flow into the entrance in the closest possible pack. The crowd dammed up outside is so tightly jammed and spreads out so wide that some impatient angels lift themselves into the air, and come skimming over the heads of the others, and lower themselves into the crowd—already thick—that is now overflowing the floor of the great hall.

THE GREAT HALL

In a few moments the hall is choked. Angels from the edges of the crowd have to move on, and pack into galleries, greatly reducing their size in order to do so.

Palace guards appear wherever necessary, constantly pressing the multitudes into galleries and staircases in order to keep the main hall clear.

High above, in upper galleries and balconies unnoticed before, some of them almost lost to sight under the towering roof, we see the foaming activity of countless figures cramming themselves in.

We have the impression of a beehive, or a bee swarm. One angel, Mulciber, transformed himself into this gigantic palace. Now the palace and all the millions of angels in it become in effect a single multicelled organism.

ONE OR TWO SIDE GALLERIES

Here the spirits pack the whole space from floor to ceiling. Latecomers, unable to find an inch of room, hover outside, fruitlessly beating their hands on the close-packed mass, pleading to be included.

INTERIOR, PANDEMONIUM

A general view of the great central space, the churning spirits now becoming hushed and still. We cross to:

THE LONG GALLERY

It now seems empty. A flicker of movement at the black pinpoint at the far end.

DOOR TO COUNCIL CHAMBER

The black pinpoint is actually a high and imposing doorway. The last few of the thousand seraphs are passing through it. We follow them in.

But far within,
And in their own dimensions like themselves,
The great Seraphic Lords and Cherubim

> *In close recess and secret conclave sat,*
> *A thousand demi-gods on golden seats,*
> *Frequent and full. After short silence then,*
> *And summons read, the great consult began.*

THE COUNCIL CHAMBER

A completely black sphere several hundred feet in diameter.

The thousand golden thrones are set widely apart in ten tiers which completely circle the middle zone of this sphere.

There is no light in the chamber except for a golden radiance emanating from the seraphs themselves—brighter and extending more widely in those of higher rank. This light is enough to show us the nearer seraphs and the golden thrones on which they are seating themselves. It illuminates little or nothing of the black substance on which the thrones are set, if indeed they are set on anything at all. Here and there we catch glimpses of the darkly gleaming interior wall of the sphere.

The luminescence is so limited that a seraph a few hundred feet away looks like only an elongated blob of light, and those farther off appear as large stars. Their brightness varies considerably in accordance with the mood and activity of the angels. Those who spring up to shout applause may actually flash for a moment. Perhaps this vast, dark sphere is Satan's brain, and the luminous seraphs are the brain cells, glowing or flashing or dimming according to the electrical impulses that pass through them.

THE ROSTRUM

A shaft of black stone rises out of the dark depths of the sphere and ends in a tiny, flat top at a level between the two lowest tiers of thrones, but a little way out toward the middle of the sphere.

A seraph is standing on this almost invisible platform. He is uttering the last sonorous but indistinct words of some formal announcement as the last seraphs enter and assume their thrones. He ceases, and disappears.

A second later, another seraph, and a larger and brighter one, appears on the rostrum. (There is no arrival or withdrawal—just appearance and disappearance.)

> SECOND SERAPH
> Our Lord, the chief of many
> princely powers . . .

He gestures to a point at a slightly lower level to his right.

SATAN AND AIDES

Satan's magnificent throne is set in the lowest circle. The thrones of his twelve great ministers are arranged in an oval whose long axis extends from Satan's throne out toward the middle of the sphere. As these highest-ranking archangels emit more radiance than the others, their luminescence merges into a single bubble of light. The Second Seraph continues without pause, each phrase evoking more and louder shouts of enthusiasm.

> SECOND SERAPH
>
> ... that led the embattled seraphim
> to war under his banner, and, in
> dreadful deeds, fearless, endangered
> Heaven's perpetual King, and put to
> proof His high supremacy.

Prolonged cheers. Satan leans toward Beelzebub, who is seated on his right.

SATAN AND BEELZEBUB

> SATAN
>
> Which, most unfortunately,
> survived the test.

Beelzebub reacts despondently. Moloch, on Satan's left, has heard and is looking savage. There is a general dimming of light among the chiefs surrounding Satan; but in the main part of the chamber the ovation continues.

SATAN AND AIDES

The rostrum is visible in the background. The Second Seraph is raising his hand, hushing the ill-considered enthusiasm.

> SECOND SERAPH
>
> Too well we see, and rue the
> dire event. Which, with sad
> overthrow and foul defeat,
> has lost us Heaven.

Cries of anger are heard on all sides.

> SECOND SERAPH
>
> And all our mighty host in
> horrible destruction is
> laid low.

He pauses; then, after a moment of silence, very solemnly:

> SECOND SERAPH
>
> As far as Gods and Heavenly
> Essences can perish . . .

Satan points with displeasure at the Second Seraph.

> SATAN
>
> *That* thought would *make* us
> perish.

He scowls. Then his light glows more intensely. He speaks in a trumpet tone, shouting toward the whole gathering.

> SATAN
>
> Mind and spirit remain invincible!

Beyond Satan we see the Second Seraph on the rostrum. He vanishes. The Third Seraph, larger and more luminous than the others, appears in his place, and is already catching up Satan's thought. He echoes:

> THIRD SERAPH
>
> . . . remain invincible!
> Strength soon returns!

SATAN AND BEELZEBUB

Satan raises a clenched hand.

> SATAN
>
> And, having returned to us,
> shall now be used.

OTHERS OF THE GROUP

> BEELZEBUB
>
> What if our Conqueror has left
> us strength, only to make us
> suffer stronger pain?

> THAMMUZ
>
> Eternal life, only to endure . . .

> ASTORETH
>
> . . . eternal punishment?

Over these speeches the radiance of the speakers and of all the others has
dimmed considerably. It begins to brighten as Satan strikes his fist on the
arm of his throne.

> SATAN
>
> Punishment!
> Talk of pleasure, rather.

> THAMMUZ–ASTORETH
>
> Pleasure? In this Hell?

> SATAN
>
> Is there joy nowhere but in warbled
> hymns? Forced praises? Servile
> offerings? And always "You! *You!*
> YOU are the highest!" Not for me!
> Find pleasure rather in what He
> forbid. Pleasures unnumbered,
> since He forbid so much.

He looks to Thammuz and Astoreth, then to others:

> SATAN
>
> Strange lusts and lewd embraces.
> Profanations. Lies, Belial,
> and deceits and guile.
> And, Beelzebub, deep-coiling
> stratagems, to tangle Him in
> His own great net of Laws.
> *Which may be done.*
> Wealth, Mammon. Wicked riches.

He addresses others.

> SATAN
>
> Above all, the sudden blow.
> Desperate chances.
> Joy in the wild attempt.
> Revenge stabbed home!

Moloch starts up, blazing with enthusiasm.

> MOLOCH
>
> New war! Open war!

As he disappears:

THE ROSTRUM

The Third Seraph has been standing there uncertainly. He now vanishes. Moloch instantly appears in his place, shouting:

> MOLOCH
>
> My sentence is for open war.
> Let us at once, armed with
> Hell-flames and fury, reverse
> our tortures into dreadful blows
> against the Torturer!

Yells of enthusiasm. Flashing lights. All around the auditorium the seraphs are blazing and cheering.

THE WHOLE COUNCIL CHAMBER

Over these speeches a reddish flush emanating from the maddened seraphs hangs like a luminous cloud in the centre of the vast, dark sphere. Soon it coalesces into a tangle of fuzzy, incandescent lines which form a fiery tracery, semi-abstract, showing an imagined assault on the battlements of Heaven.

> MOLOCH
>
> Let Him hear infernal thunder.
> For lightning, see black fire.

The fiery fantasy portrays something of these things. Faint rumblings of thunder. Moloch bellows:

> MOLOCH
>
> Let Him see with horror His
> own invented torments used
> against Him. TO BRING HIM DOWN!

A frantic ovation.

SATAN

Satan is feverishly relishing the fantasy. Beelzebub murmurs a caution into Satan's ear. Satan reluctantly accepts this. We see Moloch's vacant throne on Satan's left hand. Moloch appears on his throne, fuming.

> SATAN
>
> Strong words, Moloch!

Moloch scowls jealously at Beelzebub.

MOLOCH

But weak thought prevails!
Still I cry ACTION!
ASSAULT! ATTACK!

SATAN

Against an almighty foe?

MOLOCH

We've power sufficient to
disturb His Heaven. And with
perpetual inroads to alarm Him.

BEELZEBUB

To what good end?

MOLOCH

Not victory, perhaps, but yet
revenge.

Beelzebub makes an almost imperceptible signal to Belial, who responds with a gesture of acquiescence. He vanishes, and at once appears on the rostrum.

BELIAL ON THE ROSTRUM

BELIAL

First, what revenge? The towers
of Heaven are filled with armoured
watch that render all access im-
pregnable.

SATAN, MOLOCH, AND OTHERS

Belial's voice is audible from the rostrum, but it only becomes distinct in the passages indicated.

SATAN

Moloch, what's less than victory
is no more than loss. And if
we lose . . .

BEELZEBUB

. . . we suffer.

MOLOCH

What can we suffer worse?

SATAN

Is *this* the worst we've known?
Thus sitting? Thus consulting?
Thus in arms? We've known defeat,
and flight. What's worse than
flight?

Belial takes up Satan's thought.

BELIAL

Pursued and struck with Heaven's
afflicting thunder! We *begged*
the deep to shelter us. This Hell
then seemed a refuge from those
wounds. Were we not worse . . . ?

Astoreth rises from his throne and screams:

ASTORETH

Were we not worse, sunk in
the burning lake?

BELIAL

What if the breath that kindled
those grim fires should wake and
blow them into sevenfold rage?
What if His vengeance wakes, and
arms again His red right hand to
plague us?

MAMMON

Up there, He drowses, lulled
by chanted praise.

THAMMUZ

Or cultivates His garden.

SATAN

The Garden!

SATAN

He begins to think very intensely. A faint semblance of treetops in moonlight—a vision of Eden—begins to form in the centre of the sphere.

SATAN'S AIDES

> **MAMMON**
>
> Now He forgets us, thinking
> we still burn.
>
> **OSIRIS**
>
> He ruled that we should burn.
> Then, burn we will!
>
> **CHEMOS**
>
> Burn all that's His!
>
> **MOLOCH**
>
> Burn it with Hell-fire! Lay
> waste His whole creation!

Satan has pursued his train of thought to its end. He stands erect.

> **SATAN**
>
> The Garden! By the Heaven we've
> lost, *that's* where we strike!

On the last word, he vanishes and, in the same instant, he appears on the rostrum. The vision vanishes.

> **SATAN**
>
> Peers! Potentates! Thrones!
> Dominions! Powers! Offspring
> of Heaven! Princes, now, of Hell!

There is a breathless hush. Satan proclaims:

> **SATAN**
>
> Unceasing war!

A tremendous outburst of excitement.

> **SATAN**
>
> New war! New tactics! A new
> field to fight in!

GROUPS OF SERAPHS, INDIVIDUALS, SATAN'S AIDES

All are seen at various moments while Satan is speaking.

SATAN

Between us and Heaven lie all the
wilds of space. Where He, with
wasteful hand, wantonly spilled
out millions of new worlds.

A vision of the Milky Way floats in the centre of the chamber.

SATAN

Each with its day and darkness.
The dark for us to hide in. Strange
forms, made by His idle fancy, that
fly or crawl or run. Those forms
for our disguises. In darkness and
disguise we'll lurk, and strike.
And having struck, be gone. And
suddenly return, and strike again.

Tremendous excitement.

Moloch leaps up, shouting madly:

MOLOCH

With sudden onset! To waste
His whole creation with Hell-fire.

Satan gently represses this outburst. He now speaks slowly. He is bringing a long-forgotten episode to the surface. The vision of Eden renews itself in the centre.

SATAN

Remember now the visions we had in
Heaven. Prophetic visions that we
thought were dreams. Dreams of a
strange, small world. Two creatures
in a garden. Set there to breed, to
people all of space. And, in the
end, rise singing though the skies,
to fill *our* vacant thrones.

Cries of anger. Moloch springs up to bellow the warrior's inevitable reaction:

MOLOCH

We can destroy those frail
inhabitants.

BELIAL

Or drive them out.

SATAN

Not so! But please them. Win
them with magic spells and
practices. Until they breed
for us. Gain all their innumerable souls, and all the vast, uncertain middle of the universe.
Till we have more than He. And
thus prevail.

Wild excitement and applause.

Beelzebub, at last won over, speaks with kindling enthusiasm.

BEELZEBUB

But this is *conquest.*
This would surpass revenge.
Or mad assault against the
cliffs of Heaven.

Moloch scowls. Belial smiles.

BELIAL

And yet *include* revenge.

SATAN

Who'll find this world?

From all around the council chamber come cries of "I!" "I!" "Let me!" etc., which grow louder and more frequent in response as Satan continues.

SATAN

Who'll go through all the horrors
and the dangers of this Hell?
Who'll find the gate?
And find what guards the gate?
Outface all opposition, and
break out?
Who'll fly through night, and
chaos and the endless void?
And find this race called Man?
Who'll dare?
Who'll go?

The cries of the volunteers become deafening. Satan motions for silence. Then, with a smile of overweening vanity, he continues:

> SATAN
> None but myself shall go.

An upsurge of applause, which he again silences.

> SATAN
> Council dissolved!
> Go, friends—refresh yourselves.
> And wait in hope for what I mean
> to bring you.

DOOR OF COUNCIL CHAMBER

Satan's aides are in that same second standing in the doorway, ready to escort him. He arrives among them even as the last syllable of his speech hangs in the air. So swiftly does the fact succeed upon his thought! They form a square around him, Beelzebub on his right. Beelzebub leans to him to say quietly:

> BEELZEBUB
> Let us escort you, Lord, part
> of the way.

Satan assents. The doors open. They start in formal procession down the long gallery.

SATAN

> *The Stygian Council thus dissolved, and forth*
> *In order came the grand infernal Peers;*
> *Midst came their mighty Paramount, and seemed*
> *Alone the antagonist of Heaven.*

Such is Satan's bearing at all times. His aides are primarily interested in their duties, their careers, their sufferings, their pleasures, their rivalries, etc. Satan, like the head of a modern state, is in unremitting confrontation with his opposite and his eternal enemy. At such a time as this, when he has finally resolved on the future conduct of the war, he almost forgets his companions and, staring defiantly upward, thinks only of his ever-present foe.

Meanwhile, the progress continues.

> *. . . him round*
> *A globe of fiery Seraphim enclosed*
> *With bright emblazonry and horrent arms.*

These seraphim are six or eight of the Council of Peers, who have, like certain noblemen at European courts, a second and paramilitary function as personal bodyguards to the sovereign. As such, they are transformed into heraldic creatures, bearing shields or tabards with armorial devices, decorative weapons, etc. Those who guard Satan may transform not only their costume but also their flesh itself for the purpose. Fiery seraphim! The globe is formed by one or more of them floating in the air over Satan's head.

THE GALLERY

Satan and his entourage pass, and set off down the incredibly long gallery toward the main hall at the far end.

THE PORTICO OF PANDEMONIUM

Like bees outside a hive, a few spirits are stationed among the colossal pillars of the porch. One or two go sailing off through the air to reconnoitre the jagged mountains to the rear of the palace. Another comes swooping in from the crest of the long slope which leads up to the high skyline at one side.

The newly returned spirit speaks urgently to one of those posted by the great doorway. We are not near enough to hear what he says, but we see that he is pointing in excitement to the skyline.

SATAN AND HIS AIDES

As they emerge on to the porch. For a moment the returned spirit and the guard to whom he is speaking are out of view. A moment later we see the guard reporting the spirit's message to his superior officer.

Satan's ceremonial bodyguard divides to take up formal positions right and left of the doorway.

The officer who has the message begins to relay it to Belial.

BELIAL, THE OFFICER, THEN SATAN

The officer is speaking to Belial:

> OFFICER
> "A dreadful land," he said,
> "part fire, part ice . . ."

Belial turns to Satan:

BELIAL
> Beyond the ridge, a continent
> of horror.

Satan, who has expected nothing else, motions his aides to follow him. They set off toward the top of the ridge.

PANDEMONIUM

Satan and his aides exit. For a few seconds the face of the palace seems entirely deserted. The few guards stand motionless and dwarfed by the gigantic portico in which they stand. Then a multitude of spirits explodes out of the great doorway and pours in all directions over the terrain surrounding the palace.

THE DOORWAY

Showing the mad, demoniac energy of the young angels as they burst out of it. It is as if Satan's decision to prosecute the war has made them frantic and, at the same time, made them devilish. They behave like crowds in any capital on the day war is declared.

JUNIOR ANGELS
> War! War! War!
> War! War! War!

BETWEEN PALACE AND MOUNTAINS

Bare and rugged ground. Outcroppings of rock. Crevasses. Stretches of hot alkali.

The crowd, drunk with excitement, is flooding over all this area. Enormous leaps. Somersaults. Wrestlers fling each other in fantastic arcs. Rocks are torn up and flung almost out of sight into the air, and caught by others as they come down. Wrenching up another rock, an angel uncovers one of the great scorpions of Hell, which he delightedly seizes and flings for one of his companions to catch. More highly organised mock battles are being staged on various of the flatter spaces.

Meanwhile, the great seraphs, too dignified to indulge in such horseplay, are wending their way in groups toward the mountains. At one time or another we see them passing through or behind the boisterous crowds. Now we see that they are entering the gloomy gorges and deep ravines where the mountains open onto the plain.

A GROUP OF SERAPHS ENTER A VALLEY

What appear to be trees are pinnacles of porphyry or basalt. A number of natural rock slabs and ledges roughly approximate scattered seats in an amphitheatre. The band of seraphs, numbering a hundred or so in all, winds among the rocks. It divides into smaller groups, of about six here and ten there. There are also a few solitary figures. They arrange themselves on the natural seats among the rocks.

A SEATED SERAPH

His eyes are on the ground at his feet. This noble creature has too lofty a mind to be carried away by the unthinking exuberance of the lesser angels on the plain. Homesick for Heaven, he is thinking of the way the revolt was planned; of the high hopes at the beginning; of the heroic deeds and the final defeat and the terrors of the fall. As he remembers all this, a thin and melancholy but sweetly musical sound mingles with his sighing breath. At first scarcely audible, it soon swells louder and louder. Soon it is taken up by another seraph seated not far away. Then another voice joins in from a different quarter, and another—until the whole band is singing in wild and sorrowful and thrillingly beautiful chorus.

> *Their song was partial; but the harmony*
> *(What could it less when Spirits immortal sing?)*
> *Suspended Hell, and took with ravishment*
> *The thronging audience.*

THE THRONGING AUDIENCE

Up from the plain, crowding among the rocks at the entrance to the valley, numbers of the lesser angels, their faces still flushed and raddled by their violent, intoxicated celebration, but now strangely moved, half stupefied, half woebegone, at the sound of the singing.

AT THE TOP OF THE RIDGE

Satan and his companions arrive at a point just under the skyline. Satan motions the others to halt. He steps up to the crest of the ridge, and stands staring at what he sees beyond the dizzy precipice that falls away on the far side.

HELL AS AN ASPECT OF SATAN

The wide and gloomy expanse below the ridge, with its ghastly lights and cavernous shadows, offers a fleeting image of Satan's own face, distorted by the *thought of lost happiness and lasting pain.*

But, since Hell is conceived primarily as a place—*such place Eternal Justice had prepared for those rebellious*—the view that it is made by Satan in his own image is already disintegrating.

HELL AS GOD'S CREATION

What seemed like highlights on Satan's reflected face are seen to be burning mountains, or distant glittering peaks of ice. Flesh tints are the yellows of poisonous, sterile clays or smouldering deserts. Shadows are black towers, sinister pits, patches of dreadful night. The brow and the disordered hair are now revealed as the rocky dome, miles wide, which roofs in the infernal hemisphere and which is here and there concealed by streaks and drifts of sulphurous or of fiery cloud. But behind, below and beyond this concrete and stable place of torture, lies yet another state of existence.

THE LIMITLESS HELL OF SATAN'S IMAGINATION

Sometimes uncertainly perceived, sometimes more real and vivid than God's own creation, sometimes gone altogether, its desolate immensities and its nightmare detail are forever being created and re-created in Satan's paranoiac mind.

THE THREE ASPECTS OF HELL SEEN SIMULTANEOUSLY

This stupendous scene is not confined to a single plane. Sections of it float high in the air, like mirages. They drift apart, or they collapse, leaving great gulfs through which new visions rise up and spread out before us.

SATAN AND HIS AIDES

They have launched into flight through these fragmented and interpenetrating worlds. They alight momentarily in landscapes inhabited by monstrosities. Some of these are imprisoned in muttering pinnacles of rock. Others whirl past in the form of dust devils, startling us with sudden furious vociferations. A deep hole in the ground, its crinkled lip reminding us of human flesh, houses some unseen being who curses or complains unceasingly.

A series of such insane and nightmare visions follow one upon another with bewildering speed.

AN IMMENSE WASTE

The group is flying over an endless, half-frozen tundra, an indigo desolation.

Far ahead, we see a vivid crimson thread snaking a narrow way across this featureless waste. It is a river. It is running toward the red patch of sky arched over the lake of fire somewhere behind us.

THE RIVER PHLEGETHON

We arrive simultaneously with Satan and his aides, at the very instant they touch the ground; their bodies in the posture of swift arrival; their hair and garments still streaming behind them or falling into place.

They are standing a little distance from the edge of the river. A rocky, shaley bank slopes down to the level of the stream.

The river is of molten lava. It hisses and crackles as it flows. The force of its current rushing over its rocky bed produces a sound like the snarl of a furious beast.

Satan is disgusted, and some of the others are dismayed, by the spectacle of a river behaving like a maddened animal. Moloch, however, is stimulated by it. His eyes light up; he bares his teeth; he runs down the bank; he bends over the torrent. His face is reddened by the glare.

SATAN

Watching Moloch; calling down to him:

SATAN

What river?

MOLOCH ASKS THE STREAM

He so exactly echoes Satan's question and tone that it could be said that this is Satan speaking through Moloch.

MOLOCH

What river?

At once a fury, a dreadful creature, more or less human in form, but all fire and fangs, lifts its head and arms out of the roaring current, clasps Moloch, and hisses and growls two rapid phrases into his ear. Moloch shouts each of them back to Satan as he hears them.

MOLOCH

Phlegethon!
River of rage.

The fiery creature again approaches its mouth to Moloch as if to say something more. Instead, it bites his cheek. The next moment it has released him and disappeared into the raging torrent.

MOLOCH

Still crouching, he lifts his face, marked by the bite. His face is inflamed with a feeling at once furious and sensual—the drunken joy of wrath.

SATAN

His hand touching his own cheek. A startled look, as when a man experiences a savage and discreditable sensation, and is uncertain as to whether he enjoys it or hates it.

SATAN AND AIDES

Moloch is joining them. They are on tiptoe, ready to take off again.

TUNDRA AND PHLEGETHON FALL APART

An arctic world, with peaks of snow and glittering pinnacles of ice, breaks up through the existing scene as if it were so much torn paper. The peaks and pinnacles spread apart right and left, leaving in the middle:

AN IMMENSE WASTE OF SNOW

With snowy mountain ranges on one side; some of the white mountains being also volcanoes in eruption. Far away on the other side, the glittering pinnacles of giant icebergs. Between mountains and icebergs, endless miles of lifeless snow.

Satan and his companions are skimming over the snow. A river like a black thread meanders through this white desolation.

THE RIVER STYX

Its water almost level with the dead, flat waste of snow which extends on all sides. Satan and his companions are standing a short distance from the stream. Belial has already run to the edge. He now bends over the water.

BELIAL

The water is black as jet. Thin cakes of rotten ice float just beyond the clear patch through which Belial is trying to see into the depths. Something pale is rising from below.

    SATAN

    What river?

The pale object is a face, somewhat resembling Belial's own beautiful but hateful face, and wearing the most malign and repellent expression that can be achieved. As Belial bends lower this face rises to meet his as a mirrored image comes forward to meet the approach of the object reflected. The meeting point is not at the surface of the stream, but some inches above it.

    BELIAL

    What river?

The face, breaking through the surface, utters an inaudible syllable. Belial calls it back to Satan.

    BELIAL

    Styx!

The creature below clasps two white arms about his neck and drags his face down to meet its own in a poisonous kiss. It sinks into the depths. Belial raises himself a little and looks back toward Satan, his face reflecting much of the malignity of the creature that has just kissed him.

    BELIAL

    River of hate.

He starts toward the others.

As they take flight, the snowy waste falls apart. Satan and his aides sweep forward, and are gone.

THE RIVER COCYTUS

It flows out of a range of gloomy mountains, and through a gorge between vertical cliffs of black basalt or gabbro. It is a turbulent river, pouring into cataracts and waterfalls, sometimes flowing in stretches of deep, dark and smooth water, then foaming over jagged rocks. Large slabs of black rock overhang the steep banks. Here and there are miniature beaches and backwaters, with eddies, trickles, the lapping of ripples.

Satan and his companions are alighting on one of the great shelves of rock near the edge of the torrent. The sound of the rushing water rises higher. The fiends look at each other in astonishment and uneasiness and, at the same time, in mounting excitement. The many sounds of the river, great and small, begin to be distinguishable as sounds of lamentation; weeping, wailing, moaning, sighing, sobbing; cries of fear and pain and woe, uttered by men and by women and by children. Some are lamenting alone. Others are crying in families, in tribes, in whole nations. It is a symphony of sorrow. Its instruments range from the piercing shriek of a single napalmed child to the muted dirge of the hundreds marching to the gas chambers at Buchenwald, to the desperate clamour of the multitudes blinded on the outskirts of Hiroshima.

SATAN

Standing a little way back from the edge of the stream, watching his companions as they scatter along the edge of the water. His expression changes to correspond with the mood of each one he watches. He first looks toward Beelzebub.

BEELZEBUB

Beelzebub, with a sombre, intellectual curiosity, is bending over a very small patch of water which lies below a boulder, and which is calm except at moments when a wave breaks over the rock. He is immensely interested in distinguishing the separate cries and sobs which combine to make the generalised sound of the rushing water. Listening with Beelzebub, we hear it more clearly. Beelzebub looks back to Satan with an expression loftier and more terrifying than Moloch's savagery or Belial's venom. Beelzebub wears that look of intellectual detachment common to those who advise the murderers of mankind.

BEELZEBUB

Seen closer as he bends lower to the stream, and enquires, echoing Satan:

> BEELZEBUB
>
> What river?

A curl of water breaks over the rock. It displays a fugitive resemblance to the face we associate with classical fountains and river gods—wide mouth, weeping eyes, etc. This face utters a few syllables in a voice too broken and tearful to be distinctly audible. But Beelzebub, being closer, catches the sound and calls it back to Satan.

> **BEELZEBUB**
> Cocytus.
> River of lamentation.

Hearing this, Satan listens more closely to the sounds coming from the river. He finds himself oddly disturbed. Fated to cause pain as well as to suffer it, he is also capable of responding to it in more ways than one.

Satan walks closer to the water and along the bank in the direction of a waterfall. On the way he passes several of his companions.

SATAN AND BEELZEBUB

Beelzebub finds himself at once fascinated and annoyed by the importunate clamour. To protect his little patch of calm water from the ripples that break over the rock, he puts his hand and much of his arm into the water at surface level to make a breakwater. The moment the water is smooth an agonised face rises from below, bubbling out cries of grief and pain. This face is wholly human, unlike that of the spirit of the river. Beelzebub recoils a little, lifting his arm, and the face immediately disappears below the troubled surface. Beelzebub masters his repugnance and tries again and again. Each time a different mask of misery and a different sound of grief.

Satan moves on.

SATAN, ASTORETH, AND THAMMUZ

A little farther upstream, Thammuz and Astoreth are bending over some shallows. Thammuz scoops up some of the vociferous water in his cupped hand. With a conniving glance at Astoreth, he holds it up to his face to listen more closely. The sound seems to float off this handful of water like steam from a cup. Thammuz turns his ear to take up the sound, which here is the thin pleading and sharp outcry and painful gasps of young girls ravaged in the Dionysian revels. Thammuz licks his lips and gives Astoreth a conniving glance of approval.

Satan goes on.

SATAN AND BELIAL

Belial is even more avid. Kneeling on one of the little beaches, he has put his face down to the water and, protruding his lips to the utmost, he is sucking up the dolorous liquid as if he can never have enough of it.

SATAN ALONE

Leaving his companions bent over the stream, Satan walks along its edge. He is in profound and troubled thought. Now and then a movement of his eyes in the direction of some peculiarly poignant cry from the stream betrays the source of his disturbance.

Soon the sound of the water becomes even louder and more varied.

SATAN AT WATERFALL

Long streams of white water plunging into a deep, black pool. Rocks protrude here and there from the cliff behind the falls, catching the water at odd angles, sending out a rainbow mist at one place, making a miniature cascade at another; in short, producing the widest variety of water formations and water sounds. Satan listens intently, catching every nuance. He has participated in the different reactions of each of his followers—each of the baser sides of his nature. Now his reaction is more complex. He is overwhelmed by the unfamiliar sensation of pity, which he at once transmutes into a gust of rage. Rage against the fate which has doomed him to be the cause of all this suffering; rage against those who suffer; rage against the pain he feels when he realises their pain.

In his fury, he snatches up a large boulder and dashes it into the pool.

Like tears, always more copious than expected by those who cause them, a huge fountain splashes up and showers down over Satan, veiling him with innumerable droplets, each trailing its piteous diminuendo of wretchedness.

Satan, with a convulsive gesture, motions to the others to join him. They are instantly at his side, and they follow him closely as he soars straight upward.

THE ROOF OF HELL

Having lost sight of Satan and his aides, we view them again after a moment of searching the gaps in the sulphurous clouds which obscure much of the rocky dome that is the roof of Hell. Now they are flying in close formation, following the curve of the roof, looking no bigger than a flight of hornets in the dome of the Pantheon.

THE ROOF OF HELL

Now closer, and above the clouds. We see the rough arch of the roof, with strata broken off, stalactite formations, ledges notched in, shallow caves, etc.

Satan and the others are scouring along far ahead of us. We see them land on a rocky platform deeply recessed into the great dome, at more than three quarters of the way to its highest point.

HELL GATE

Over a rough but flat floor of rock, a cave, hundreds of feet wide, hundreds of yards deep. Its roof is an arch of rock. Natural buttresses thrust out here and there on either side. At other points, huge boulders have fallen from the roof. This gigantic cavern tapers to what will prove to be, when seen closer, a most stupendous gate. In form, this gate will follow the line of the uptilted curve of this high latitude in the hemispheric dome of Hell.

Satan and his companions, having alighted on its lip, now advance into the cavern, and see the gate.

A NEARER VIEW OF HELL GATE

Satan and his followers have now come near enough to see that there is a rock protruding as a natural seat on either side of the gateway. On each of these seats a creature is sitting. At the sight of these two creatures Satan's companions stare, hesitate and slow their pace. Soon they fall away from their leader one by one, and slip into shelter behind boulders and buttresses and in fissures in the walls of the cave.

Satan undauntedly advances toward the gate.

The figures on either side of the wide gate are looking toward each other. Thus each is presenting only a profile to Satan. Even when they take cognizance of his approach, they turn their heads only a little to regard him. When they do this, and at all times during the present encounter, nothing of the other profile is visible to us. It is as if blacked out, not there.

As he approaches them, Satan looks first at the monster seated on the left-hand side of the gate.

SIN

Sin is the feminine principle of evil. It is necessary for her to be beautiful—otherwise she would be powerless—but her beauty is ravaged and repellent. She is withdrawn, pale, cold, venomously hostile, and full of frigid lust.

Sin looks with peculiar intensity at Satan, but does not move.

We are now aware that the other creature has risen and is advancing upon Satan.

DEATH

> The other Shape—
> If shape it might be called that shape had none
> Distinguishable in member, joint or limb,
> Or substance might be called that shadow seemed,
> For each seemed either—black it stood as Night,

> *Fierce as ten Furies, terrible as Hell,*
> *And shook a dreadful dart; what seemed his head*
> *The likeness of a kingly crown had on.*
> *Satan was now at hand, and from his seat*
> *The monster moving onward came as fast*
> *With horrid strides; Hell trembled as he strode.*

Death is a whole complex of shapes. At any time he may thrust forward the face of one of his many forms, and each time this aspect seems almost to be the whole creature. All the other forms are subdued into a substance like that of a jellyfish or hydra, restlessly writhing and undulating like a living cloak around the dimly seen central figure, which wears the kingly crown. This central figure is the essential and abstract Death—implacable, majestic, terrifying and beautiful.

SATAN AND DEATH

Satan is not merely wondering at the extraordinary and ever-changing shape of his formidable challenger, or the dark central core where the kingly crown is fitfully seen, or the constantly emergent dart. He wonders most of all at the colossal insolence of this creature who opposes himself to one who, apart from the Trinity, is the noblest and most puissant of the lords of the universe.

Death, still a pace off and a little to Satan's right, shouts from out of the heart of his undulating substance:

> DEATH
> No farther, Satan!

> SATAN
> What now? What's this?

Stepping squarely in front of Satan, Death brings him, astonished, to a halt.

> DEATH
> I am the end.

> SATAN
> The end? A miscreated monster . . . ?

> DEATH
> Of *your* creation, Satan.

Death's voice is so cold and commanding that Satan restrains his impulse to thrust the monster aside.

> SATAN
>
> My creation? Who *are* you? *What* are you?

One of the writhing coils of jellylike substance shoots out like a fleshy stump, like a neck with a face spreading on the end of it. The face is hideously blotched and discoloured, like that of one dying from a virulent plague. This dreadful face thrusts itself close into Satan's face, and yells—or gasps, or hisses:

> THE FACE
>
> Plague.

At the same time, Death shoots out his flickering dart from the mass behind, its tip nearly piercing Satan's left side. Satan drops his left hand onto the dart, thrusting it down and away. Simultaneously he slashes his right hand across in front of him, striking the face, which distintegrates. The neck contracts like a wounded tentacle, and withdraws into the main body.

Satan addresses the very dim figure within the mass.

> SATAN
>
> You hide within yourself,
> and send a slave to speak
> for you. Who are you,
> coward?

At this insult, Death becomes furious.

SATAN AND DEATH

Death grows *tenfold more dreadful and deform.* As he towers up, the rocky vault of the cavern loses almost all its substance, and it seems as if these giant opponents are standing on an endless barren waste, under the wild sky of the limitless Hell.

SATAN

Satan has grown in size to match Death, and *like a comet burns, that from his horrid hair shakes pestilence and war.*

> DEATH
>
> Back to your punishment!

SATAN AND DEATH

> *such a frown*
> *Each cast at the other as when two black clouds,*
> *With Heaven's artillery fraught, come rattling on*

> *Over the Caspian, then stand front to front*
> *Hovering a space, till winds the signal blow*
> *To join their dark encounter in mid-air.*

The wild sky over these two towering monsters reminds us for a moment of the mad, furious, agonised reflection of his own face which Satan saw when he first looked over Hell. Satan and Death are grappling inside this huge, vague representation of Satan's head. Satan's voice sounds like the rumble of thunder; Death replies like the single sharp explosions sometimes heard in a thunderstorm.

> SATAN
> First, say your name.

Death thrusts forward a horribly wounded face at Satan, and again lunges at him with his dart.

> DEATH
> Murder.

Satan, with a sound of rage and contempt, again dashes the dart aside and strikes at the menacing face.

Now the action accelerates, and at the same time the struggle becomes huger and more obscure. It is more and more like a battle between thunderclouds, with the thrusting dart, like flashes of forked lightning, illuminating the ghastly faces that Death thrusts forward, and with the voices rumbling and exploding like thunder.

At one moment or another we hear Satan shouting:

> SATAN
> What are you called?
> Who are you?
> Say what you are!
> Your name! Your name!

Between these shouts Death is replying as loudly:

> DEATH
> Famine.
> Fever.
> War.
> Fire.
> Despair.

Other stricken faces are thrust forward; other names of Death are thundered out. And always the lightning flicker of the stabbing dart, and Satan sweeping it aside and striking the faces out of existence. At last Satan thrusts his arms elbow-deep into the mass and seizes the throat of the central figure. As he chokes it, all the subsidiary forms fall limp and lifeless.

SATAN AND DEATH

Simultaneously, Satan and Death are reduced to their original size, and their setting is again the rocky shelf in front of Hell gate. The central, kingly aspect of Death becomes clearly visible as Satan cries triumphantly:

> SATAN
>
> Now we discover who and what you are.
>
> DEATH
>
> Know me, then! I am Death!

As he speaks he strikes again with his dart. Death is now unhampered by his fallen disguises, which hang about him like rags. The dart pierces Satan deep under his heart. Blood flows down Satan's side. He feels the deadly pain, and staggers, but he does not fall.

DEATH

He in turn stands disarmed—his dart being sunk in Satan's body—and amazed. He watches as Satan, with intense pain, grasps the dart with both hands and tears it out of his flesh.

SATAN AND DEATH

Satan has drawn out the dart, but still stands uncertainly, trying to recover his strength. Death steps forward and seizes the dart. Satan tightens his grip. They struggle. Death tears the dart from Satan's hand and lifts it, ready to strike again. Satan draws back to launch a counterblow. Sin's voice is suddenly heard:

> SIN
>
> Hold back that dart!

SATAN, DEATH, AND SIN

She rushes between them, seizing Death's dart in her left hand, and pushing Satan back with her right, in which she holds the large and elaborately formed key to Hell gate.

All three struggle. All three are breathless. Their words are rapid, broken, overlapping each other. Sin cries first to Satan:

> SIN
>
> My father, and my lover, hold
> your hand!

And then to Death:

> SIN
>
> See where you've wounded him
> who gave you life!
>
> SATAN
>
> You call me *what?*

The physical struggle is suspended. Satan and Death await Sin's reply.

> SIN
>
> I called you Father.
> And he, your son and mine.
>
> SATAN
>
> That phantasm my son?
> And you, seen close, more
> hideous than he.

He stares at her with increasing repugnance.

> SIN
>
> Have you forgot me, then?
> Am I so changed? Remember now
> that day the first small thought
> of planned revolt entered your mind.

Satan is sufficiently impressed to try to remember.

> SIN
>
> Then your eyes dimmed. Your
> head near burst with pain.
>
> SATAN
>
> This head never felt pain in
> Heaven. Once, a slight, agree-
> able dizziness—music in the brain.

SIN

From that head I was born! Full grown! A goddess! And they called me—Sin.

Satan shakes his head, smiling scornfully.

SATAN

Sin, I remember well—her loveliness—which all adored who saw her.

SIN

You most of all, who made of me your love.

SATAN

That face Sin's face?

SIN

You held me to your heart.

SATAN

Never!

SIN

To you I bore him. Death! Our dreadful son.

SATAN, SIN, AND DEATH

Satan is incredulous. Yet he is troubled. He scowls. He attempts to push past.

SATAN

Enough of this imposture.

Death steps into his path again, raising his dart, stabbing.

DEATH

Enough, indeed!
Back, Satan, to the fire!

SIN SCREAMS IN FURY

SIN

Will you still fight like

fools? Then know for whom you
fight. For Him who sits above
and laughs at both. You, Satan,
cannot die. But yet can feel
the stab. And Death, appointed
to devour all living things . . .

DEATH

Still starves.

SIN

Save for a few poor weeds of life
which grow untended on unheard-of
worlds.

DEATH

Light, soulless stuff which cannot satisfy.

Satan thinks deeply for a moment, then speaks with an appearance of concern. For the first time we see Satan the tempter.

SATAN

You starve, my son? And you,
Sin, grow weary here on guard
where no one knocks for entrance.
Let me go out. I go to find a
world where there's to be a race
of upstart creatures. There you
shall find welcome, and many
lovers, Sin.
And Death shall find his prey.

SIN

Here is the key of Hell.
But I may use it only to
let in.

SATAN

Letting me out, you will let
millions in.

Sin and Death exchange a long look. Death nods. Sin hesitates. Satan takes the key from her and crosses to the gate.

SATAN

He steps up to the lock and inserts the key.

HELL GATE

The turning of the key starts an immense and complex mechanism. The ninefold gate opens first this way and then that, always starting a more ponderous unfolding, until at the very end a great section of the rocky crust of Hell falls down like a drawbridge, becoming an extension of the rocky platform within, and stretching out into blackness and nothingness.

At the conclusion of the unfolding of the gate, Sin and Death stand facing each other on either side of the gateway.

As if a flue had been opened, the glare of the fires deep in Hell begins to increase.

SATAN

He now strides straight out through the gate and to the edge of the platform. Without looking back, he raises his hand in a brief gesture of farewell, and disappears.

HELL GATE

Seen from halfway down the approach to the gate.

First Moloch, then Beelzebub, then, one by one, all the rest of Satan's aides come cautiously out of their hiding places.

We follow Moloch as he passes through the gate. We notice that, though he bears himself erect, he is careful to keep to the exact middle of the gateway.

HELL GATE

As Moloch passes through, we see that Sin and Death have now taken seats outside the gate corresponding in position to those inside. Since we follow Moloch toward the gate, we see only that profile of each that we have seen before.

BEELZEBUB AND OTHERS

Beelzebub now passes us, and goes through the gateway, also keeping carefully to the middle. The other aides follow, mostly singly, Thammuz and Astoreth together. All display the same more or less controlled fear of the terrible figures that watch them as they pass through.

THE OUTER EDGE OF THE PLATFORM

Satan's aides gather there. They are staring upward, all scanning the same arc of the sky.

THE SKY

High up on the opposing arc there is a long tangle of stars—a Milky Way miniaturised by distance. Something is passing between us and the stars of this distant universe, blotting out section after section as it passes.

We see the heads and shoulders of some of the group as they point and stare.

> BEELZEBUB
> See where he flies!

> BELIAL
> There!

> MOLOCH
> There!

Astoreth has glanced back toward the gate. He clearly has no wish to pass again between the terrible figures that guard it.

> ASTORETH
> And there we'll follow.

> BELIAL
> Intrude upon his errand?

> MAMMON
> Not I.

> CHEMOS
> It could offend him.

> DAGON
> "None but myself," he said.

Astoreth again glances back at the gate. Thammuz shares his feeling.

> ASTORETH
> But await him at a distance.
> There to welcome his great
> return.

THAMMUZ

And bring him home in triumph.

THE AIDES

Something less than a glance—an electric wave of assent—passes through the whole group, and they simultaneously lean a little forward as if to take off, and in that instant they vanish.

AMONG THE STARS

We are traveling with, or just behind, the swift fliers. Sometimes one or another, or a number of them, comes between us and some shining constellation.

At other moments, one or another of their faces, already ashine with their mounting luminescence, sails for a brief space close across our field of vision.

Soon we see Orion, the Great Bear, the Pleiades and other familiar constellations.

THE GREAT SQUARE OF PEGASUS

Into this large, dark space, a meteor falls—and stops in mid-air, still shining. Another and another swoop down to join it.

THE GROUP

Three or four of Satan's aides have already chosen their places and sit there, comfortable in mid-space, their hands locked around their knees. Others are in the act of sweeping in to join them, and squat or sprawl or recline, or link arms like double stars, and all together form a group, rather like the Pleiades, shining brighter than they did in the council chamber.

Having arranged themselves, they look to where Satan flies, and we look with them.

THE STARRY SKY

Stars and groups of stars still being blotted out.

We fly in pursuit of this dark ripple in space, and find it to be a rush of darkness formed like an arrow, black against the dark blue of night.

APPROACHING THE SUN

Riding on that wave of darkness, which is Satan in flight, we become aware of light flooding in from some as yet invisible source. Wheeling down toward this light, we sweep far ahead of Satan, and discover the sun.

THE SUN

Ptolemy's sun—a brilliant, golden disk of very limited size, which circles the Earth.

THE ARCHANGEL URIEL IS STANDING IN THE SUN

In this intense light and heat, his giant form seems to be made of molten glass. In height, Uriel is somewhere between a fifth and a tenth of the diameter of the sun. He is a little less than Satan is in his natural shape, and considerably more than Satan is in the disguise Satan will assume. His face, like those of all good angels, is entirely unmarred by the stresses of thought or sorrow or experience. His calm and radiant beauty is as perfect as a classical mask.

Uriel stands, at once vigilant and relaxed, watching over the Earth far below.

THE EARTH

A wide curve of its surface, much as seen from a modern satellite. Mesopotamia is in the centre of the curve exposed to us.

URIEL AND THE SUN

Behind Uriel, and to his left, the dark wave that is Satan comes sweeping in. Satan emerges out of this darkness; it drops off him like a cloak as he lands on his feet near the rim of the sun, and behind Uriel.

URIEL AND SATAN

Uriel senses the intrusion, but it takes him a moment to withdraw his watchful gaze from the Earth. In that same second, Satan reduces his stature to that of the most junior of angels.

As Uriel turns to look at him, Satan completes his disguise by drawing a mask down over his face.

Uriel, seeing Satan, sees the youngest, freshest, most enthusiastic fledgling angel that can possibly be imagined—a student cherub seeing the universe with the help and the good will of his seniors. Uriel looks with some little surprise at this arrival, and good-humouredly beckons him to approach. Satan obeys.

> URIEL
>
> What strong wind blew *you* out
> so far from Heaven?
>
> SATAN
>
> The great, warm gale of God's
> own will, Lord Uriel.
>
> URIEL
>
> With His own breath He scatters
> out His songbirds?
>
> SATAN
>
> A few of us. Millions still pack
> the choirs, bursting with songs
> of praise.
>
> URIEL
>
> Unwearying voices!

Uriel's eyes turn often to the Earth. He does not hear Satan murmur:

> SATAN
>
> And an unwearied ear.

Uriel looks back at Satan.

> SATAN
>
> Some, like myself, whose voices
> are uncertain, were bidden fare
> out through these new-made heavens.
> To hear what songs the suns sing
> in their circling. Or gather, in
> the flowering fields of stars, new
> praises for their Maker.

URIEL

How if some strong and evil spirit,
caged there below, should break out
of his prison?

SATAN

Heaven forbid! And,
Heaven forbidding, how
could one escape?

URIEL

Ask me no mysteries. The order
was to stand here. Here I stand.

SATAN

Guarding the Earth! And that
new wonder—Man!

Uriel grunts assent, and looks steadfastly at the Earth. Satan, standing beside him, peers in the same direction.

SATAN

If I could see him, what I'd
have to sing of!

URIEL

Look along my spear.

As Uriel points his spear and Satan sights along it.

THE EARTH AS SATAN SEES IT

URIEL

To right and left—two seas.

SATAN'S FACE

He is narrowing his eyes.

PART OF THE EARTH

Lesser features become clearer as Satan peers harder and harder.

SATAN

Two seas?

URIEL

One dimmed already with
advancing night . . .

SATAN

And one still gold!
I see them!

URIEL

Between them, a land . . .

SATAN

Yellow, and dead, and dry.

URIEL

Two rivers . . .

SATAN

Winding like serpents.

URIEL

And where they nearly join . . .

SATAN

What seems to be a cloud.

URIEL

Look closer yet.

SATAN

Trees! High-towering trees!

URIEL

Those trees hedge in the Garden.
Eden. That's his home. There's
two of them now. One's what they
call a she.

SATAN

And may I go there?

URIEL

To find a new song? Yes, child.

SATAN

Such as you've never heard, I
do assure you.

Satan turns, ready to take off. Then he turns again, respectfully supplicating what he knows will be granted.

SATAN

First, your blessing.

URIEL

Whatever's sweetest and most
precious there, keep the thought of it close to
you always.

Satan, with a gesture of gratitude and reverence, dives into space. Uriel watches.

SATAN FLOATS DOWN

Seen by Uriel, Satan floating gently down with the lightness of a leaf or a butterfly. His form becomes much diminished by distance.

URIEL

Smiling benignly as he watches. He allows himself to look upward for a moment as if in gratitude for this refreshing visit.

SATAN IN SPACE

Still in the form of the young angel, he floats lightly down on a wide spiral.

He hooks his thumb under the chin of his mask. He rips it off. He reassumes his giant magnificence. The minnow turns into a pike. He thrusts *his steep flight in many an aery wheel*. It is a frenzy of exultant triumph. On a last wild sweep, he swings down out of sight. A bright speck is left floating in mid-air.

THE BRIGHT SPECK

It is the mask. It wobbles gently in the air, smiling vacuously up toward the sun and Uriel.

URIEL

Looking down again, he sees the last of Satan's furious swoopings as the latter disappears into the Earth's atmosphere. Uriel is mildly disquieted. He tries to shrug off his misgivings.

SATAN AND THE EARTH

Hundreds of miles below him, Satan sees the Earth in its entirety. He reaches out his hands as if to seize it.

PLAINS AND MOUNTAINS

Part of the plain of Mesopotamia, facing north toward Mt. Niphates and the ranges behind it. From Niphates, long ridges run onto the plain. These are forested to a height of several thousand feet. Above this, bare rock, and, on the peak of Niphates, snow.

NIPHATES

Showing the peak, and the bare crest of the highest of the ridges, and, as we look upward, the sky over it.

High up, Satan dives into sight, at first as small and swift as a darting hummingbird, but quickly growing in size and speed and menace as he swoops down.

MOUNTAIN PEAK AND RIDGE

Satan lands high up on the ridge, near where it springs out from the mountain a few hundred feet below the snowline. He comes toward us with large strides, looking keenly about him. He halts, and gazes out over the plain.

THE GARDEN OF EDEN AT A GREAT DISTANCE

We can just see the enormous trees that hedge in the Garden, and the two rivers converging.

SATAN

His eyes are on the Garden. He decides to watch it for a while. The mountainside is broken by cliffs and escarpments, some of a size to make a seat for Satan. He sits. He rests his elbow on his knee and his chin on his hand. His other hand rests on the ground beside him. His eye falls on the area immediately in front of him. On the face of a rock, he sees patches of lichen. In cracks and veins in the rock some simple mosses and dwarf saxifrages have found a precarious roothold. Below Satan's feet is a little gully where a scree begins, and in its gravel some sort of high-altitude scrub is barely existing. We see an empty snail shell, bleached by long vacancy; some scraps of the shed skin of a viper caught between tough stalks; the breast feather of a falcon—altogether a thin and brittle blueprint of life. Unlike the rich life of Eden between the two rivers, this is a vagrant, accidental sort of existence; spare, austere, delicate, lovely. A sort of life, one may fancy, that first drifted to this mountaintop as spores blowing in with the interplanetary dust.

SATAN

His fingers encounter a little patch of moss. He tears up a square inch of it, and holds it on his palm. The moss seems like a mere speck on his giant hand. Satan narrows his eyes on the moss.

THE MOSS

The tiny filaments, the two or three minute, starry florets, a bud or two—all as seen by the magnifying eyes of Satan.

SATAN

He reaches for the snail shell, for a harebell or a heath flower, and then for the falcon's feather. All these examples of Earthly life are of absorbing interest to him—they are existences of an order he has never encountered before. He feels a peculiar kinship with them. These things have evolved from the dust of the angels atomised by God's thunderbolts.

SATAN'S PALM

And the feather on it. Satan breathes on the feather. It floats away.

SATAN

He watches the feather float down. He reaches for it. A little eddy in the air twists it beyond his grasp, and it falls where a thin, flat rock juts out to partially cover a little depression in the ground.

Reaching again to recover the feather, Satan encounters yet another new thing—an egg. It lies in the little hollow under the rock. Satan forgets the feather and takes up the egg. It is a very small, roundish, whitish egg. Satan is fascinated by this ultimate simplification of the forces of life and growth.

Suddenly the descending sun clears an overhanging cliff and sends an intrusive ray to spy on the treasure in Satan's hand.

Satan looks up in anger. He sees or imagines Uriel detecting him. He turns his hand over, and slaps the egg flat on the rock. It is crushed under his hand.

Careless of this, Satan rises and sets off down the mountain, in the direction of the flat land below and the distant Eden.

ROCK AND BROKEN EGG

The creature within it, almost ready to be hatched, lies dead and exposed. It is not a bird, but a viper.

URIEL

Riding the sun, he peers hard to make out exactly what is happening on the spur of Niphates. But the sun is already in swift descent into a golden sunset, and the area he is watching is soon lost to his view.

BETWEEN NIPHATES AND EDEN

The land is mostly bare and eroded yellow clay. Patches of scrub here and there, thorns and thistles, and now and then a ragged palm tree or parched live-oak.

Satan comes striding through this semidesert. In relation to earthly objects, he is about forty feet in height. When at their full stature, all angels, whether fallen or not, look as if they are coated with some opalescent substance. Thus they seem a little less substantial than human beings, and more beautiful. On entering the Garden, however, they reduce themselves to human size, and their flesh seems darker and denser and more ordinary.

BOUNDARY OF EDEN

Cedars of Lebanon, heavily foliaged pines, ilex, an undergrowth of laurel, box and myrtle make a dense hedge. In some places an almost vertical outcrop of rock towers up behind or in place of the trees.

Satan comes up to the hedge of trees, which are more than twice his height. He springs easily over their crowded crests.

HEDGE OF EDEN, INNER SIDE

Satan lands lightly on his feet. He recovers his balance, and at once diminishes his size. He steps into the deep shade of the wide belt of woodland that girdles the Garden. He disappears among the trees.

THE GARDEN OF EDEN

A magnificent parklike landscape with wide stretches of grassland grazed down to lawns; superb specimen trees, profound woods, scattered groves and copses. Various fruit trees clustered in thickets or standing alone. Sooner or later we shall see signs of a little primitive cultivation: a plot of tillage, a retaining wall upholding a terrace, a basin in the process of being carved from a stone which juts out under a spring.

Various decorative birds and animals, half tame, are grazing in the open, or peeping from the wood's edge. Deep among the trees we see the glowing skin of a leopard recumbent on a level branch.

A little track skirts the curving edge of a massive woodland. We hear voices. Adam and Eve are walking toward us.

ADAM AND EVE

These two are to be the ancestors of all mankind. Between them, they carry the seeds of all the physical and mental characteristics of future races.

Adam's strain will predominate in those who spread north and west from the Caucasus. He is a splendid specimen of this northern type: upright, fair-haired, broad of brow; a believer in natural law and divine order, in duty, reason, honest toil and unquestioning obedience. Even so, he ultimately proves capable of the most romantic loyalty and Quixotic sacrifice.

Eve is all that Adam is not. She is a woman. Moreover, hers is the strain from which spring all the southern and eastern races; all the darks and the golds of Africa and Asia are mingled in her colouring. She is a creature of feeling and instinct, dreams and visions; troubled by vague longings and disturbed by potentialities unrealisable in her present blissful existence.

Before we can distinguish the words, we detect a question in her voice. Now they are close enough for us to hear Adam's answer.

> ADAM
>
> We rake them up, and pile
> them in heaps.

> EVE
>
> And what becomes of them then?

> ADAM
>
> You've not been here long enough
> to know. They rot down and dry
> out, and they become dust. The
> rain washes it into the river.
> The river bears it out of the Garden.
> Or the wind blows it away. What more
> can you ask?

> EVE
>
> Then they're not seeds any more.

> ADAM
>
> Only dust.

> EVE
>
> If we let them lie where they fall?
> And grow?

> ADAM
>
> I've been told not to.

> EVE
>
> Yes, but if?

Adam smiles indulgently.

> ADAM
>
> *"If!"*

Eve has to laugh at her own naïveté. Adam explains:

> ADAM
>
> We'd have trees beyond number.
> They couldn't grow. There'd

> be no room for them, and soon
> no room for us.

They pass on. An unassuming bush in the near background, which they have almost brushed in passing, drops a slender branch of foliage not dense enough to hide a rabbit, and—behold!—we have been staring at Satan all the time.

As soon as Adam and Eve are out of sight, Satan turns and makes a bound into the shelter of the wood.

ANOTHER PLACE ON THE WOOD'S EDGE

Here the track is narrowed by encroaching briars or the like. Adam walks a little ahead. Eve, following, looks through a gap in the wood's edge, and sees something which fascinates her. She halts for a moment.

Adam's voice comes comfortably from two or three paces ahead of her.

> ADAM
> Come, Eve!

Eve hesitates so briefly before obeying that we barely realise she has hesitated. She herself probably does not realise it. Satan, however, does. We now see he is lying in another impudently exposed ambush, and as Eve passes on he takes a long look at the object which made her linger that moment after Adam called her.

THE TREE

The Tree of Knowledge of Good and Evil stands alone at the end of a little glade. It is obviously a very special sort of tree. Its main branches rise from a central trunk and curve outward and downward like the water of a fountain. Its Fruits glow like jewels amongst the glossy foliage.

After a long look at the Tree, Satan looks after Eve as she follows Adam.

Soon he plunges back into the wood, and hastens along a parallel path until he is ahead of them again.

EVE OVERTAKES ADAM

He speaks in a tone so free from reproach that it reminds us of reproach.

> ADAM
> You know . . .
>
> EVE
> I know.

ADAM

That Fruit is not for us.

EVE

I know.

ADAM

I only want you to be happy.

ADAM AND EVE AND SATAN

As they walk, they constantly uncover Satan in a new camouflage. Sometimes he lurks behind a screen of leaves at the wood's edge; sometimes he walks with unbelievable effrontery almost at their elbows, stepping half a pace aside with perfect timing just as a head is turned, protecting himself at other moments by lifting his little twig with half a dozen broad leaves on it, and so forth. He reacts with lively intuition to all the implications in Eve's vague hints of unrealised longings. Adam and Eve walk along by the wood's edge, then follow the path through an outlying copse.

Their conversation continues without pause.

EVE

I *am* happy. I don't think I
could be happier. It isn't that.

ADAM

Then what is it?

EVE

If I knew!

ADAM

It's a joy to know what you are
thinking. When you can tell me.

EVE

Often I can't tell you.

ADAM

Then it's wonderful *not* to know.
There has to be light and shade.

Eve looks at Adam.

EVE

Sometimes just plain brightness—like the sun.
That's best of all.

After a pause, she says:

EVE

Adam . . .

ADAM

Beloved?

EVE

I don't want that Fruit.

ADAM

We have everything else.

EVE

Yes, we have.
Everything else but that.
Why think of it?

ADAM

All the other fruits. Flowers.
The birds.

Pressing aside a branch, he steps out of the copse into a clearing.

THE CLEARING AND THE BOWER

A large outcrop of rock has a nearly vertical side. The bower is set against this, not far from where the path comes out of the copse. The roof and the two ends of the bower are made of a trellis of split chestnut saplings. The roof over the area where they sleep may be thatched with reeds, and the trellis at that end may be reinforced with the same material, as a protection against wind and rain. The bed inside, and a low table and couple of seats outside, drinking gourds, etc., should be such as would be made by an intelligent man whose needs are so simple that he has never had to invent any but the most primitive tools. Thus he can chop poles and split them, but he can't fell a tree or saw boards. No animal skins are used, but bark, basketwork of osiers, rushes or palm fronds, large flat stones, etc., serve for all purposes.

The front of the bower is mostly open, and the whole thing is pleasantly overgrown with sparsely flowered vines.

The path has come out of the wood at an acute angle, and runs close to the edge of the wood for some little distance in the direction of the bower.

Satan is soon to be seen, sometimes behind Adam and Eve, sometimes a little ahead of them.

Adam's last speech was uttered as they emerged from the wood. He continues without pause.

ADAM

The little animals you love
so much.
More love, I sometimes think,
than I can spare them.

He shows her the branches and undergrowth at the edge of the wood.

A number of small creatures are living a semidomesticated life at the edge of the wood. A squirrel, a monkey, a lemur, an ocelot and the like are peeping out at the humans. Eve puts her hand out to touch one of these. It draws back an inch into the criss-cross of branches. Eve cannot reach it.

EVE

If we *really* had them!

ADAM

But here they are.

EVE

I *look* at them.

As she speaks, walking along, she flutters her fingers in the air as if touching an invisible barrier. The movement may suggest what would be—if it existed—a shop window.

EVE

But something . . .

ADAM

When they eat from your hand?
When they all know you, and
wait for you?

EVE
> But have them for my *own*. In a way that . . .

Adam, scratching his head, looks at her, trying to understand. Eve, unable to formulate her thought, makes an instinctive movement. She cradles her right forearm in her left, holding her right hand to her left breast. The discontented girl doesn't know what a baby is, but she wants a baby.

THE VISITATION

Suddenly the scene is lit by an illumination much brighter than the bright sunshine. The source of this dazzling light is descending from the sky and into the woods a little distance away. As it comes down it emits such a blaze that all shadows race around into realignment, and Adam and Eve, turning to look, clap their hands over their eyes.

In the same moment, Satan leaps in a tremendous arc through the air, and dives at the juncture of the rock mass and the level ground on the farther side of the bower. He plunges head first into the rock, and is gone.

Adam and Eve cautiously peep through their fingers. The great light is now among the hundred-foot-high cedars of the deep woodland.

THE GREAT LIGHT IN THE WOODS

Adam and Eve see an oval shape nearly forty feet high and eight feet through at its centre. It is now on the ground at a distance of two or three hundred yards, and framed by the tall trunks of the cedars and the wide black levels of their branches. It has already lost much of its unbearable brightness, and it is shrinking in size. Its outline is indenting a little at points corresponding to where a human neck and waist would occur.

ADAM AND EVE

Their different reactions. Adam realises that this must be an ambassador from Heaven. He recovers sufficiently to welcome the illustrious visitor with great respect and simple dignity. Eve feels all the wonder and reverence appropriate to seeing such a glorious being. Adam at first draws her forward by the hand, and then, when she has regained control of herself, he sees to it that she walks in seemly fashion close behind him toward the archangel.

THE ARCHANGEL RAPHAEL

By this time the great pillar of light has contracted to the size and form of a very tall and outstandingly beautiful human. He smiles graciously as Adam comes gladly toward him, followed, at the correct distance, by Eve.

We observe that in the presence of a third person Eve's subordinate position becomes much more noticeable.

> ADAM
>
> Heaven's ambassador?

> RAPHAEL
>
> There called Raphael. Sent
> you by God to share your evening
> meal.

Adam motions Raphael toward the bower, eager to entertain his glorious visitor.

> RAPHAEL
>
> And talk with you on matters of
> great moment.

TABLE OUTSIDE BOWER

The talk is in progress. Adam sits at a right angle to his guest. His manner is hospitable, attentive, respectful—a barbarian chief entertaining a Roman consul.

Eve does not join in the strictly masculine conversation. Much of the time she is bringing more fruits to add to the positive cornucopia on the table or replenishing the wooden cups from various long, bottle-necked gourds. When she is not thus occupied, Eve seats herself on a low seat beside Adam. While she is sitting there, she is a married partner, though a humble and a silent one, listening in awe to what the great ambassador is saying to her husband.

When she is bringing more food and drink, passing behind the two males, and sometimes standing with a hand on her hip, Eve is less a wife than a serving maid; less a reverent listener than an eavesdropper. In this situation she is free to indulge in a private opinion, and to express it with a smile, a sceptical look, or a frown.

> RAPHAEL
>
> Keep in mind, Adam, your great
> happiness.

Eve is at this moment crossing from her seat to get something for the table. On the word *happiness* Adam's eyes find and follow Eve. Raphael watches Adam, noting his fond expression. Raphael's own expression is eloquently inscrutable.

> ADAM
>
> I know it well.

> RAPHAEL
>
> And know to whom you owe it?

Adam glances again toward Eve, then back at Raphael.

> ADAM
>
> And thank Him—every hour.

> RAPHAEL
>
> Know this besides. He sent
> me here to tell you.

He is delivering an official admonishment. A raised finger.

> RAPHAEL
>
> It's in your power to keep your
> bliss, or lose it. Obey or dis-
> obey—you're free to choose.

Adam sits bolt upright as if to emphasise the correctness and the earnestness of his reply.

> ADAM
>
> To God, who gave that freedom,
> I give, with all my heart,
> obedience.

Eve is listening to this speech. She feels that Adam should not have to make such a very formal declaration of his love and gratitude. But her expression changes as she sees:

ADAM

He is seized with a vague but painful misgiving. He looks searchingly at the beautiful, majestic, blank mask of Raphael's face. He asks anxiously, almost sharply:

> ADAM
>
> He, who knows all, He knows
> *that,* does He not?

> RAPHAEL
>
> What He knows, He knows.
> All *I* know is, to warn you
> of your peril.

Eve is not pleased by what she overhears, or by the sight of Adam's struggle to grasp all the implications.

> ADAM
>
> He knows what I will do . . .
> yet sends to warn me?

Eve suspects a trap, and fears that Adam is too honest and too reverent to perceive it.

> ADAM
>
> But if He knows that I will
> stay obedient, what need to send?
> And if—God forbid—He knows
> I'll disobey, what use? What use
> in sending?
>
> RAPHAEL
>
> This use—that if you wilfully
> transgress, you shall
> not now pretend to have
> been surprised by evil,
> not forewarned.
>
> ADAM
>
> Forewarned of what? Of whom?
>
> RAPHAEL
>
> Satan. God's enemy.

Eve has set the fruit on the table, or refilled the cups, and now unobtrusively takes her seat at a low place. She fixes her eyes on Raphael with the look of a peasant woman who feels her husband is being given a hard deal. Raphael continues without pause:

> RAPHAEL
>
> Once called Lucifer. Greater
> than I; greater than all in Heaven,
> save God and God's own Son.
> But envious, proud, and lawless,
> full of hate and wrath, he could
> not bear God's Son's preeminence.
> Thus moved, he made revolt—
> revolt against God! And hence
> was smitten, overwhelmed, cast

down to Hell—he and his
millions—there to lie, prisoned
in torments, burning without end.

Raphael pauses and drinks. He relishes the flavor.

Eve leans toward Adam and, considerably disturbed, whispers a question to him. Raphael, seeing this, sets down his cup and looks enquiringly at Adam, who is somewhat embarrassed.

ADAM

She wants me to ask you—
were all those millions of bright
angels doomed to burn forever?

RAPHAEL

Being disobedient, yes. Beware
of him who brought this fate upon
them.

ADAM

But if he's thus conquered, and
imprisoned . . . ?

RAPHAEL

Adam, in Heaven there is one power
alone. That power is God's great
will. On Earth, the force which
flares in the lightning flash pervades all being. It holds together
particles infinitely small; lights
thought throughout the mazes of the
brain; orders and animates all things.
In Hell, there's a power which, being
in essence evil, is by its nature unknowable to Heaven. By this accursed
force, this power of magic, Satan has
raised himself and all his band out
of the burning lake.

ADAM

Ah!

RAPHAEL

He—the arch-fiend—has
broken out of Hell. Uriel,

>   who guards this Earth, today has
>   seen him. It may be in his
>   mind to enter Eden and bring
>   about your downfall.

SATAN'S EYES

They are glowing at the juncture of rock and ground.

ADAM, EVE, RAPHAEL

Adam indicates Eve.

> ADAM
>
> She sometimes dreams some
> monster waits to devour me.

> RAPHAEL
>
> The woman's dreams? Froth of
> disordered fancy. God's command
> is first to *you*.

> ADAM
>
> And I resolve to obey. So
> what's in doubt?

> RAPHAEL
>
> Yourself. Being changeable.

He very delicately, and with infinitely faint distaste, indicates Eve.

> RAPHAEL
>
> And this a creature incom-
> plete, and most imperfect.

Adam delights Eve by venturing to protest, and sturdily.

> ADAM
>
> But given me by God, Lord Raphael.
> Who, while it seemed I slept, opened
> my side. He drew from me that rib
> which lay closest my heart.

Raphael is listening politely but without any sign of sympathy. Adam sets his hand on Eve's neck, proudly, to display her.

ADAM

And formed and fashioned it
until she grew so lovely that
all she does and says seems
wisest and most virtuous and best.

RAPHAEL

Seems best! A mere outside?
Had not His greater wisdom
sanctioned it, I'd say this
carnal love was a device made
by His enemy.

Eve is deeply wounded and insulted. She turns her face away. Adam actually interrupts the seraph.

ADAM

Am I not to love her sweetness
and her goodness?

Raphael rises. He raises his hand high, towering over Adam and Eve. They have not time to get to their feet, though they try to. When Raphael speaks, Adam and Eve remain motionless, half risen, half crouching in front of him.

RAPHAEL

Adam, beware! Love no one more
than God. Obey no other, or be
lost for ever.

RAPHAEL

He begins to grow taller and to blaze with light. He is on the way to becoming that forty-foot, blinding incandescence we saw descend from the sky. Already the sight is too bright for human eyes to bear. Turning from it, we see the nearly dissolved silhouettes of Adam and Eve, their hands clasped over their eyes, as they wheel away from the intolerable light and fling themselves on the ground. In doing so, they turn toward each other.

ADAM AND EVE

Pressing their faces down as the great light begins to lift. Adam's head is not far from Eve's. He ventures to pull one hand away from his tightly shut eyes and fling his arm over Eve.

The light begins to diminish. Soon it is gone. Adam and Eve remain prostrate. After a long pause they get up, silently, and cross toward the bower.

EVE

He told you not to love me.

ADAM

Not more than God, he said.
That love is not the same.

THE BOWER

Adam begins to clean off his tools. The head of his mattock is blunted. He strikes off a few flakes of the stone to restore its edge. Eve arranges her cups and platters.

EVE

"A creature incomplete!"
"A mere outside!" How did I
offend him?

ADAM

It may have been wrong to ask
about the angels. Or wrong to
let your fancy stray in dreams.

EVE

But if I can't help it?

ADAM

I was never told not to. But yet
I've the feeling it's better that
we don't. So I . . . no longer dream.

EVE

I know. You've told me.

Adam's face is inclined upward as he calls to mind and quotes:

ADAM

A sound, healthy, and refreshing
sleep.

EVE

I try.

She begins to smooth the low, mossy couch which is set against the rock at the other end of the bower. Adam, finished with his tools, soon crosses toward her. Close to the head of the bed, and just beyond the roof line, a small bush is growing. It was behind this bush that Satan dived into the rock.

ADAM

All things *do* sleep at night.

EVE

The night bird sings.

ADAM

If you were asleep you wouldn't hear it.

SATAN

Satan has thrust his head and shoulders out from the rock at ground level just behind the bush. Resting on his folded arms, he has been listening to the discussion with intense interest.

EVE

But when I sleep, I dream.

GABRIEL'S COMMAND POST

It is a lightly constructed pavilion with most of one side open to the air. We shall see that it is set against one of the great outcrops of rock that in places wall in the Garden. Close at hand is a wide cleft in the rock. This forms the western gate of Eden.

The Archangel Gabriel is one of the greatest commanders of the Heavenly armies. At present he is taking his ease, which is interrupted by the hurried entrance of an adjutant.

>ADJUTANT
>The sun's on the very point
>of setting, General.

>GABRIEL
>Uriel signals all's well?

>ADJUTANT
>No signal yet.

Gabriel at once rises and moves toward the opening.

>GABRIEL
>Is there yet time for the flash?
>Let me see this.

Shouts are heard from outside:

>SHOUTS
>He's here!
>Tell the general he's here!

Gabriel is now in the entrance.

> GABRIEL
>
> The archangel has come here?

GABRIEL'S PAVILION AT DUSK

As Gabriel comes out. Two junior officers have shouted, and they now point to where Uriel attends.

Uriel and Gabriel hasten toward each other.

> GABRIEL
>
> We watched for your last sign.
> Instead, we have yourself.
> This is a pleasure.

> URIEL
>
> *My* pleasure, Gabriel—once
> my mind's at rest.

Gabriel speaks in a lower tone.

> GABRIEL
>
> Something amiss?

> URIEL
>
> An hour ago, I had a *visitor*.

Pause, and an exchange of glances.

> URIEL
>
> The least and youngest of
> Heaven's choristers.

> GABRIEL
>
> So far from home?

> URIEL
>
> He had a story, which, *if* it
> was true . . .

> GABRIEL
>
> Tell me inside. You've signaled
> Heaven, of course?

Uriel nods. Gabriel steers Uriel into the pavilion. We see them seat themselves, leaning their heads together, talking inaudibly and with increasing concern. Beyond them, we see:

OUTSIDE THE PAVILION

The youth of Heaven, private soldiers off duty, playing their evening games, and, behind them, the gate.

GATE OF EDEN

Angels now on duty are posted there as a more or less formal guard. But the gateway itself is rendered impassable by the Sword of God, an electronic barrier which appears and vanishes and reappears at tremendous speed, sweeping and flaming over every inch of the wide gateway.

ENTRANCE TO PAVILION

Gabriel steps out, now extremely martial. Uriel is close behind him. Gabriel calls:

> GABRIEL
>
> Uzziel!

At once his adjutant is facing him.

> ADJUTANT
>
> General?

> GABRIEL
>
> Take half our men. Patrol the
> outside of the Garden. Be sure
> no spirit of evil worms his way in.

The adjutant at once turns and shouts for the company to fall in. A touch of military briskness, but, like the armour, scanty and only decorative.

Gabriel makes a short, cordial, and reassuring gesture to Uriel. Uriel gestures thanks and farewell, and vanishes.

> GABRIEL
>
> Ithuriel! Zephon!

He crosses rapidly toward the Gate. The two tall and experienced veterans he has summoned are with him when he halts there.

GATE OF EDEN

Gabriel, Ithuriel, Zephon. Gabriel turns to the other two.

GABRIEL

Into the Garden itself!
No common spirit can have
ventured in. And yet—
who knows?

Gabriel steps close to the gateway, and, with upraised hand, into the path of the Sword itself, which stops for him. Ithuriel and Zephon hasten through, casting awed glances at the powerful phenomenon arrested for their benefit.

GABRIEL

Once inside, diminish to the size
of those you guard, as all their
visitants do.

As they enter, Gabriel calls after them:

GABRIEL

Make sure the pair are safe.

He turns to where his company is lined up.

ITHURIEL AND ZEPHON

Now diminished to six feet high, they glance at each other, and then, in considerable awe of their surroundings, they advance into this very sacred and forbidden retreat, never seen before by any angel except God's special representatives.

The moon is just rising over the trees.

THE BOWER. ADAM AND EVE ABOUT TO SLEEP

ADAM

One simple rule to keep.
And given all this happiness.
Is it not worth while?

EVE

Indeed it is. I can't understand
what makes me . . .
I'll never speak of it again.

ADAM

Nor dream of it, I hope.

SATAN'S HEAD AND SHOULDERS

He is leaning on his folded arms, more or less in shadow at the foot of the rock. He hears Adam's last words, and smiles. After a few moments of thought, he decides on his course of action. The shape of his head begins to change.

A PATCH OF MOONLIGHT

The light falls through a gap in the boughs and onto the ground immediately in front of Satan's head. Satan has changed himself to something indistinctly seen in the shadow, but which now crawls forward into the moonlit area. It is an enormous toad. The toad crawls on in the direction of the low couch.

ITHURIEL AND ZEPHON

As they walk farther into the Garden. Ithuriel is looking around him with great interest. He sees a little patch of cultivated ground and indicates it to Zephon. Zephon nods, but duty prevails over curiosity and he hurries Ithuriel on. Pointing ahead along the path where we saw Adam and Eve, he says in a low voice:

> ZEPHON
>
> This path will lead us to them.

ANOTHER PART OF THE GARDEN

We are at the edge of a wood consisting mostly of enormous cedars, with an undergrowth of exotic shrubs bearing white and glistening flowers. Shafts of moonlight create a dreamlike effect, which becomes stranger and more sinister as we watch. The nightingale has been singing unobtrusively in the previous shots; its note now rises to that disturbing insistence which may intrude into a feverish dream.

Between the trunks of the tall trees we see a ghostly figure intermittently visible as it approaches through alternating moonlight and moonshadow.

EVE DREAMING

Pale, walking like a somnambulist, Eve comes through the wood, and out of it into the full moonlight. A pale, nacreous gleam on her flesh suggests that this astral body is of the stuff which not only dreams but also angels are made.

THE TREE OF KNOWLEDGE

Eve sees it when she comes out of the wood. She moves toward it. As she does so, she appears less ghostly than before. She seems to breathe in new life from the Tree itself.

THE BOWER

Adam and Eve are sleeping inside, almost entirely hidden by the shadow of the trellis above. But Eve is closer to an outer corner, and the moonlight falls through to show us her head.

The large toad is now sitting close to Eve's head, whispering into her ear.

THE TREE

The wonderful Tree is itself alive. A tremendous force is beginning to surge through it. More and more, as the scene continues, it lives and burns and shines and sings.

EVE AT THE TREE, AND SATAN

She approaches haltingly. Satan meets her, seeming to materialise from the Tree itself.

Eve looks at him in wonder, but also with that unquestioning acceptance with which we greet the marvellous apparitions that occur in dreams.

> SATAN
>
> Fair Eve, you know me.
>
> EVE
>
> You must be one of those who
> speak with Adam.
>
> SATAN
>
> Thus far—you know me.

Eve's happy assent shows how he is leading her thoughts.

He draws her toward the Tree.

> SATAN
>
> Come close. Fear nothing.
> This Tree and you, the loveliest
> things in Eden—made by the same
> hand, were they not?
>
> EVE
>
> But Adam's forbid to taste.
> One came today . . .
>
> SATAN
>
> To you?
>
> EVE
>
> No. Not to me. He had no
> word for me. To Adam, though,
> he brought a stern reminder.

84

SATAN

> Good Raphael! He's stern. As
> often those who serve are sterner
> than their masters.
> Look at me, Eve.
> I am, I think you see, a something
> greater than that messenger.

Eve's eyes are held by Satan's. Her face floods with awe and rapture. She timidly nods.

SATAN

> As you yourself shall be . . .
> when you taste this.

He offers her the Fruit. She hesitates, trembling. Satan's arm presses more closely around her shoulders. The force and music in the Tree grow more and more potent.

EVE

> But Adam . . .

SATAN

> Sleeps. A sound, healthy, and
> refreshing sleep. Heaven will
> bless that sleep. But you, dear
> Eve—in this your innocent
> dream—may innocently taste.

He touches the Fruit to Eve's half-reluctant lips and, with a seducer's smiling pressure, forces her to taste.

Eve feels the intoxicating effects of the Fruit. She looks at Satan with sad and loving reproach. The music from the Tree grows yet keener and more thrilling. The trees in the surrounding glade are beginning to assume a luminous life of their own.

SATAN AND EVE AS THEY RISE

Her head is level with his breast; her feet a little lower than his. They begin to rise, very slowly at first, into the air.

It seems to Eve that her blood is singing with the Tree. She is aware of the percussion of her quickened heartbeat.

SATAN AND EVE OVER EDEN

Now they are above the billowing, moon-silvered treetops. We hear, woven into the music, the croak of the tree frog, the droning flight of the beetle, the whirr of the wings of the hawk moth, and other nocturnal sounds.

> EVE
>
> Why do they sing so loud
> tonight, the frogs?

As she speaks, she looks down. It seems Satan has lent her his unlimited power of vision, for her glance darts through:

UPPER LEAVES

With the moonlight on them, but becoming translucent, transparent, and finally invisible as we look.

BELOW THE LEAVES

Twigs and branches, on one of which is a small, green tree frog, his throat distended like the cheeks of a trumpeting angel. We hear his triumphant song.

> SATAN
>
> They've a new goddess whom
> they celebrate.

BRANCHES AND TREE FROGS

Behind the first criss-cross of half a dozen branches, we see many more, and more tree frogs on them, and more and more and more branches and tree frogs—all the leaves and branches and tree frogs in Eden, all chorusing their joy in what is happening.

> EVE
>
> The moth sings to the flower.

As she speaks:

A HAWK MOTH

The almost blur of its incredibly rapid wings as it hovers in front of a flower into which it thrusts its long proboscis.

EVE

She is in an ecstasy.

> EVE
>
> And, hark!—the flower is
> singing to the moth. How
> sweet it sings!

EVE AND SATAN

Satan bending his head, looking at Eve's rapturous face. He is delighted by her. They are now rising high above the Garden. They look over its boundaries and see the wide spread of yellow desert. At a great distance, something visible only as a black spot.

> EVE
>
> Is that the world outside?

> SATAN
>
> Where creatures, great and
> small, pass life from one
> to the next.

He indicates the dark spot in the distance. Eve sees with Satan's far-ranging vision:

A LION

—with its paw on a dead gazelle, looking up with its yellow eyes at Eve.

> EVE
>
> One lies so still.

> SATAN
>
> Taken by Death.

> EVE
>
> Death? What's that?

> SATAN
>
> The end of such poor creatures.
> That weak life, without a soul,
> now goes to the other. Who in
> turn will die. Thus the wild life
> goes on.

SATAN AND EVE STILL HIGHER AND THE WORLD BELOW THEM

Now so high that we can see beyond them: on one side the snowy peaks of the Caucasus, and on the other the waters of the Indian Ocean sparkling under the moon.

> SATAN
>
> See where the great whale swims!
> See the monsters in the deep
> of the sea!

WHALES

First one and then a school, wallowing and spouting. They sound, and as they go down we go down with them.

> SATAN
>
> Bred of the stuff of angels,
> those whose dust, scattered
> by God's great bolts, blows
> through the universe. The
> seeds of unhallowed life!

SQUID, RIBBON FISH, AND OTHER GROTESQUE SEA FORMS

Blotted out by a cloud of luminous shrimp which rises from the deeps and spreads over the screen.

THE SKY

The shrimps are, after all, stars. Satan and Eve rise among them.

> EVE
>
> Look! Look at the stars!

> SATAN
>
> And hear them sing.

The music of the spheres.

> EVE
>
> Look at the fire-folk sitting
> in the air!

A CONSTELLATION

Much like the Pleiades, only twelve in number.

SATAN'S AIDES

Reclining, much at their ease, and in the full blaze of their beauty, waiting for Satan.

> EVE
>
> How lordly! How glorious
> they are!

> SATAN
>
> My friends and my companions.

SATAN AND EVE

> EVE
>
> Angels of Heaven.

Satan sets his lips and makes no reply. Eve looks up.

> EVE
>
> And there, high in the sky!
> It gleams! It shines!

Her finger traces a long line. We see this long golden line only while looking with Eve. Satan looks up, narrowing his eyes, but sees nothing. He is surprised and deeply disturbed by the fact that Eve can see what he now cannot see.

> SATAN
>
> You see the cliffs and walls
> of Heaven itself?

> EVE
>
> Do *you* not see them?
> You, who come from Heaven?

Satan studies Eve's face. In it, he studies her soul. He sees how to appeal to her.

> SATAN
>
> I reigned there once, a prince.
> I was called Lucifer, son of
> the morning. He who rebelled
> against injustice.

Eve looks at him in wonderment, and soon in pity.

> SATAN
>
> Conquered and condemned. Sent
> down in fires to suffer.

> EVE
>
> Ah! Poor Angel!

> SATAN
>
> Down there.
> You see that redness there?
> Eternal fire!

The red glow from Hell gate becomes increasingly visible at a vast distance below.

> EVE
>
> I see a gate.

> SATAN
>
> Guarded by monsters.

> EVE
>
> Monsters? Those two?

> SATAN
>
> Sin and Death.

SIN AND DEATH SEEN BY EVE

It is the hitherto unseen side of each that is visible to Eve. With her, we see two figures of great majesty and great beauty. Sin cradles something in her arms, the nature of which becomes clear only when Eve speaks of it.

> EVE
>
> No. But that one—a woman
> like myself.

> SATAN
>
> A woman of a sort. And one who . . .

> EVE
>
> But she is beautiful.
> What's that she has at her breast?
> *I* know their names.
> Those there are *Love* and *Birth*.

Shaken to the roots of his being, Satan looks at Eve in rapture, like one awakened to a new and thrilling view of things. Eve is in a transport.

> EVE
>
> I name new things, as Adam
> named the beasts. "Love!"
> "Birth!"

She touches her cheek.

> EVE
>
> What's this? What happens to me
> now? O, Angel, this is weeping.

She raises her tear-stained face to Satan. He touches a finger to her cheek, and then to his lips. To the taste of the tear he reacts with wonderment, and a solemn relish. He looks at Eve with an extraordinary mixture of love and cruelty; joy and sorrow. She looks back at him with equally contradictory feelings: hopeless trust and beautiful foreboding. Satan begins to bend his head down toward Eve's. He is going to taste more of her tears; kiss her cheek . . .

PATH THROUGH COPSE

It is the end of the path that opens on the bower. Ithuriel is halted in mid-stride; one hand back to arrest Zephon, the other holding his spear, pointing it—

EVE

As she lies sleeping, and the toad with its mouth at her ear. In the next instant Ithuriel has stepped forward and touched the toad with the diamond point of his spear.

THE TOAD

The toad disappears in a soft flash, much like that given off by a handful of loose gunpowder when ignited. A column of dark smoke hangs in the air. It is rapidly transformed into the formidable figure of Satan.

THE SKY

A bright meteor slides down the sky and falls into the woods where the glade and the Tree are situated.

SATAN, ITHURIEL, ZEPHON

> *Back stepped the two fair angels, half amazed*
> *So sudden to behold the grisly king.*

The smooth and identical masks of the two angels are in sharp contrast to the dark and ravaged face of Satan, which, in this moment of shock and fury, shows all its livid scars. The two angels realise that this can be none other than Satan himself, but they feel so much awe of his earlier greatness and so much distress at seeing him as the arch-enemy of God, and now in ruin, that they have difficulty in facing the situation.

Zephon says falteringly:

ZEPHON

Who are you?

Satan advances his face a little. It is now less ravaged than it was a moment before.

SATAN

You know me well enough.

They are compelled to nod or murmur agreement.

SATAN

But you I do not know.
Nor care to know. Who sent
you here to spy and to intrude?
Go back to him.
I'll follow.

Zephon and Ithuriel turn to lead Satan to Gabriel. Satan follows with the air less of a prisoner than of a commander. For a moment the path and the surrounding trees are deserted.

PATH AND TREES

These now undergo a change. They do not revert completely to the lush and exotic aspect of Eve's dream landscape, but they become, as it were, the ghost of it.

Eve is coming through the trees, faltering and forlorn, like the ghost of herself coming back through the fading ghost of her dream.

THE BOWER

Eve steals up to her sleeping body and re-enters it.

GABRIEL'S PAVILION

A slab of rock serves as a table. There are two or three seats, modelled more or less on Greek or Etruscan examples. Gabriel's sword belt, with sword, is lying on the table slab. Gabriel is seated near the table slab, listening in amazement to Zephon, who speaks to him in an urgent whisper, and whose limbs are arrested in the attitude of one who has entered in haste.

> GABRIEL
> Himself?

Zephon affirms, and points. Both look to:

SATAN AND ITHURIEL

The prisoner and his guard have halted a little distance away: two glimmering figures in the classical moonshade of a giant cedar.

Satan advances, smiling, very much at his ease. Gabriel rises, hastily and yet with dignity. Zephon stands at attention; Ithuriel follows Satan.

GABRIEL'S PAVILION

Satan enters. He has already seen Gabriel's belt and sword on the table slab. Before his own sword can be demanded of him, he unbuckles his belt and flings belt and sword beside Gabriel's. Satan bears the same relationship to Gabriel as a prince of the blood bears to a field marshal. That is to say, he "treats him as an equal."

> SATAN
> My dear General, I'm delighted
> to see you again.

Gabriel is delighted to be remembered and to be greeted so warmly. This upright soldier at no time forgets his own position of trust, nor Satan's great fall. However, he feels there is no harm in courtesy. He indicates a seat. He gestures to Ithuriel and Zephon to withdraw.

> GABRIEL
>
> Be seated, Prince. I have to
> tell you plainly your intrusion here
> is an offence. Which Heaven will
> much resent.

Zephon and Ithuriel withdraw. Satan sits, stretches out his legs, smiles at Gabriel, and then makes the merest permissive motion toward Gabriel's own seat, which perhaps Gabriel was going to sit on anyway. Over all this, and also over Gabriel's speech above:

> SATAN
>
> The accident of being on oppo-
> site sides has not in the least
> diminished the respect and—
> if I may say it—the great
> affection I have always felt
> for you.

The two speeches make a sort of duet; Satan's last flattering phrase emerges as a solo at the end. Gabriel is touched.

> GABRIEL
>
> Let me say, Prince, as far
> as duty permits . . .

> SATAN
>
> Duty! *That* tether won't
> stretch far.
> And I'd not have you stretch it.

> GABRIEL
>
> It's no great stretch to ask
> an old . . .

> SATAN
>
> . . . *an old friend,* you were about
> to be kind enough to say.

94

GABRIEL

To ask him how he's faring.

SATAN

Why, General, how do I look?

Gabriel looks deep into Satan's eyes. What he sees disturbs him.

GABRIEL

Changed.

SATAN

That's how I'm faring. Change
and change and change!

GABRIEL

You seem to glory in it.

SATAN

All our glory is change.
Poor imperfection *must* change.

GABRIEL

Unresting imperfection!

SATAN

And poor Perfection cannot.
A stagnant glory!

He addresses this sneer to his Enemy above. Gabriel is disturbed.

GABRIEL

I'm a plain soldier, Prince,
and . . .

SATAN

. . . and all your talk is duty.
Then tell me, General, what
are those you guard?

GABRIEL

The he and she there? You've
seen them. Like to ourselves,
yet most unlike. They stay on
the ground always. Flightless!
Their thoughts, I suppose, creep low.

SATAN

Her, I set dreaming.
She took me into her dream.

GABRIEL

You? Into *her* dream?

SATAN

So much so, the crawling thing whose shape I wore was left all senseless, and I didn't hear your heavy-footed underlings.

Satan plays with Gabriel.

SATAN

To which we owe this meeting, dear old friend.

GABRIEL

Ah, Prince!

SATAN

Prince no more.

GABRIEL

That's true, of course . . .

SATAN

Emperor now!
As you could be a king.

GABRIEL

Of such a realm?

SATAN

Better than none. And could expand . . . upward.

GABRIEL

Not so. He has set the limits.

SATAN

Set them He has. And set you here to guard them.

> And me to stay outside.
> Where I'll retire.

He rises. Gabriel at once stands up.

> GABRIEL
>
> On your parole?

> SATAN
>
> Oh, I assure you.
> And if you change your mind . . .

> GABRIEL
>
> You go back now to . . . ?

> SATAN
>
> To my companions in misfortune.

Gabriel puts his hand on Satan's sword belt as if to restore it. Satan stays him.

> SATAN
>
> Keep it, dear friend. With it, the memory of one who well remembers you. And will do, always.

He steps back, and out from under the canopy, smiles, and vanishes.

NIGHT SKY WITH STARS

Among many constellations, we soon narrow in on that one which resembles the Pleiades, and which is in fact made up of Satan's twelve aides sitting in the air. We sweep into the middle of this group, arriving simultaneously with Satan.

SATAN AND AIDES

All are looking to Satan as he appears among them, a new star suddenly blooming in the soft clear dark. They float in to form a closer circle around him. He smiles at them.

> BEELZEBUB
>
> Satan, in your eyes I see the world you've seen.

> ASTORETH
>
> A place of much delight?

SATAN

Much delight.

MOLOCH

How guarded?

SATAN

Oh, by some fellow. Some General
what's-his-name. He led the
charge on our left flank that day . . .

BELIAL

Not Gabriel?

SATAN

The amiable idiot.

MOLOCH

With what force? How disposed?

SATAN

More than he needs, and less
than will suffice him.

MOLOCH

Make riddles for the others.
Tell me straight: how many shall
I summon up from Hell? When and
where needed? When to . . . ?

SATAN

None. Never. Nowhere.

Everyone is amazed, taken aback, silent. Only Moloch, running down like a clockwork toy, continues with a few diminishing phrases.

MOLOCH

Formed in a crescent on the
edge of night. Or darted
spearlike at the . . .
No troops?

SATAN

No troops. And no assault.
And no new legions stooping down

>   from Heaven to drive us, burning,
>   down to that burning sea.
>
>   MOLOCH
>   You countermand the attack?
>
>   SATAN
>   I *make* the attack.
>
>   MOLOCH
>   But . . .
>
>   SATAN
>   Myself. Alone. And not in arms.
>
>   ASTORETH
>   You said we should seduce them.
>
>   SATAN
>   Later, Astoreth, you shall
>   seduce . . .

Thammuz opens his mouth to ask an eager question. Satan answers before he can speak. He points to Thammuz.

>   SATAN
>   . . . *and* ravish. All you will.
>   After the multiplication has set in.
>   When that small world teems with
>   their likenesses. Have them all!

An excited reaction among various of Satan's aides. He interrupts it by saying:

>   SATAN
>   All! All but one.
>   And that one you shall have—
>   as you have me.
>   I am yours, am I not?
>
>   ISIS
>   Our lord.
>
>   MAMMON
>   Our ruler.

But they are not quite sure of the implication.

BEELZEBUB

Satan, your meaning is too
deep for us.

SATAN

Yet simple.
The great and perfect Fool has
made, in His sublime unwisdom,
two imperfect things. Of these—
one snores. So much for that one!
Let him sleep for ever.
The other—dreams.

A long pause. Satan's companions look at each other, wondering what is implied by his change of tone.

SATAN

I've been her mind's inhabitant.
I know the warmth, and salt,
and surging of her blood. A
creature made only to enjoy,
enjoy! Yet hankers strangely
after some strange sorrow.

His fond and musing tone is more and more disquieting to Beelzebub and the others. Belial mutters, unheard by Satan:

BELIAL

Which we'll provide her.

SATAN

Living, she calls it. I tasted
at her eyes the wellsprings of
the last river that we saw . . .

BEELZEBUB

Cocytus?

SATAN

She named it *Weeping*. She
makes new names.

ISIS

This new-made creature names things?

> SATAN
>
> I raised her, dreaming, to the
> high zenith of creation. She
> saw you all—and thought you
> beings of glory.
> I showed her Hell gate. It seemed
> to her, she said, the gate of life.
> Seen from so far, and from the
> outer side, and through such eyes,
> indeed it has that aspect.
> Sin and Death, those dreaded
> guardians, she new-named *Love* and *Birth*.

Satan's aides are looking at each other. Their lips wonderingly frame inaudible words—"*Love? Birth?* What can all this mean?"

> SATAN
>
> Is this not one who dreams?
> One who speaks music and magic?
> One who'll use those names to
> bring multitudes in to us?

A ripple of assent and enthusiasm. All feel they have at last seen a point of practical value.

> BEELZEBUB
>
> Multitudes who, once in, if they
> turn back, will find the Guardians
> somewhat less than smiling.

> BELIAL
>
> Once in—the trap is shut.

Satan ignores Belial; explains to Beelzebub.

> SATAN
>
> Multitudes who, in her sweet
> company, will wish for no return.

Thammuz, with greedy lips, moves up to Satan.

> THAMMUZ
>
> Is she so lovely, then?

SATAN AND THAMMUZ

Satan, much gratified by the eager question, nods a lingering affirmative. Then he says decisively:

SATAN
And fit to be our queen.

SATAN'S AIDES

Their incredulous reaction. Their consternation.

BEELZEBUB
Queen?

BELIAL
Our queen?

SATAN
My queen.
And therefore yours.
Empress of all Hell.

A shocked silence. Then cold, breathless, lifeless voices:

ISIS
This Earth creature?

MAMMON
Cousin of the clay?

SATAN
Up from this clay, I assure you,
such a flower . . .

Infatuated, he expects no serious opposition. But Belial thrusts forward an insolent face.

BELIAL
Made empress over *us?*

SATAN
Who better?

A formidable confrontation. Belial backs down.

BELIAL
None better.

He turns away.

BELIAL

His back to Satan, he sourly mutters to Isis and Chemos the reverse of the words Satan has extorted from him:

102

BELIAL

Better none.

ANOTHER ANGLE

Beelzebub addresses Satan reasonably and with considerable firmness.

BEELZEBUB

Satan, we need no ruler but yourself.

SATAN

And if *I* should need . . .

Three speeches almost overlapping each other:

BEELZEBUB

You?

MOLOCH

Who'd not be ruled by God?

ISIS

Be ruled by such as she?

SATAN

Not ruled. But, understand me . . .

BEELZEBUB

But understand yourself.

Before Satan can reply, Astoreth moves forward with lifted hand, nodding assent to Beelzebub.

ASTORETH

For this is love.

SATAN

Love . . .

BELIAL

Your weakness, Satan.

BEELZEBUB

The infirmity, perhaps, of greatness such as yours.

APOLLO

The future Delphic Oracle cries out in the piercing, mad voice of prophecy:

> APOLLO
>
> God's great Son has that same failing. And one day—I see it clear—He'll bleed—He'll bleed for it.

SATAN AND HIS AIDES

Belial points to Satan.

> BELIAL
>
> Remember, all—in Heaven, his love for Sin! Which brought us ruin!
>
> BEELZEBUB
>
> Is this not one of the two set there to breed?
>
> SATAN
>
> Such was *His* will. Which to us, is . . .
>
> THAMMUZ
>
> But breed she must. Satan. She *must* breed.
>
> BEELZEBUB
>
> What multitudes come in, but of her breeding?
>
> MOLOCH
>
> Whence come my armies, if she does not breed?
>
> ISIS
>
> My priests? My incense, and my worshippers?
>
> ASTORETH
>
> My lustful bands?
>
> THAMMUZ
>
> My myriad couplings?

MAMMON

My golden images? Massy altars?
Chalices? Who'll mine the earth
for these if her brood fails us?

BEELZEBUB

Except through her, how can we
win the Earth? And then win Heaven?

BELIAL

See our great leader—stupidly
good!

Others speak almost simultaneously, moving close to Satan, ready to merge their being with his.

MOLOCH

Of enmity disarmed!

ISIS

Bereft of guile.

BELIAL

Of hate.

CHEMOS

Of envy.

BELIAL

Of revenge.

BEELZEBUB

No longer with us—who for
his sake are damned.

MOLOCH

Will you betray us, Satan?

SATAN

Never.

ISIS

Yes. For this *love.* Love for
God's new creature. Loving her,
he'll creep back into God's own
love.

BELIAL

We *are* betrayed.

SATAN

Now we see that Satan's aides are indeed embodiments of various aspects of his personality. Their faces appear, angry, reproachful, sad, inside Satan's own face.

SATAN

Not by me. I . . .

BEELZEBUB'S FACE

Then leave her, Satan.

ISIS' FACE

Abandon her.

THAMMUZ–ASTORETH'S FACES

Or else abandon us.

MOLOCH'S FACE

Abandon me—your wrath.

BELIAL'S FACE

And lose me, Satan—and lose
all your hate.

ISIS' FACE

I am your pride. Now throw away
your pride.

BEELZEBUB'S FACE

Your wisdom, and your power.

Beelzebub, regaining his own figure, spreads weak hands. Satan reflects the gesture. Satan falters:

SATAN

Let her stay there then. She
shall be our foothold on the Earth.
Our entrance into the gates of life.

APOLLO'S FACE

Satan, you shall have her in the
end. And all her daughters.

> THAMMUZ'S FACE
>
> For midnight meetings on the
> mountaintops. In secret places . . .

Suddenly the other aides assume their separate entities.

> BELIAL
>
> Spoil her, Satan. And leave her.
> And on the scent of her corruption
> we'll come wheeling in, and . . .

Beelzebub takes Satan's hesitation for assent. He confirms the commitment by reassuring the others.

> BEELZEBUB
>
> This way our Lord will let us in
> upon the world, and . . .

DAGON

A warning shout from Dagon:

> DAGON
>
> Daylight!

He is pointing to:

THE EASTERN SKY

Largely filled with the great black curve of part of the Earth. Over the edge of this curve, a tiny, silvering rim of light. This light slowly seeps into the darkness, paling the stars.

> MOLOCH
>
> Dim down your brightnesses!
>
> BELIAL
>
> Or that bright Eye will dim them.

SATAN AND AIDES

Their luminosity is fading. Several look at Satan with lingering distrust. The emergency forces him to resolution.

> SATAN
>
> Down, then, all of you! And
> there await me. I'll follow
> darkness round, and, at the

chance, stoop to this Earth and
fix my hold upon it. And call you
all to tear it. And devour.

DAGON

Down!

SATAN

Down!

All his aides swoop down like rockets into the depths of space.

SATAN

Hanging in darkness like a surfer awaiting the wave. The light increases. Satan flings himself into the deep night as it draws back around the Earth, and sails in orbit, *following darkness like a dream.*

SATAN RIDING THE NIGHT

Satan, sometimes at a great distance, like a satellite, is swinging around the Earth in opposition to the sun, where Uriel is still standing sentinel.

Satan, floating lazily in the sapphire blue of night, sometimes insolently lags until the reddening dawn can be seen behind the ragged treetops on some Earthly mountain range. Then, with tremendous impetus, he shoots ahead of the threatening sunrise.

At other times, Satan boldly advances to the edge of sunset, where, adroitly avoiding the last of its rays—splayed out into space like the spokes of some enormous wheel—he studies the surface of the Earth. At last, he sees the spot where the river Tigris pours into a cavern at the foot of a cliff, with two tall cypresses growing on its edge. Satan hangs motionless until night has again overtaken him, and then:

SATAN

He falls like a meteor from the midnight sky.

CLIFF AND CAVERN

It is the cliff already seen by Satan, with the two tall cypresses growing above, like horns, and the river pouring into the wide cavern below.

METEOR

The meteor which is Satan streaks down from the sky and splashes into the water at a considerable distance upstream.

SATAN

Just visible in the dark torrent as it pushes past and plunges into a subterranean gulf inside the cavern. We hear the angry roar of the waterfall.

Satan's movements are not those of an ordinary swimmer, but lunging motions like those of a pike as it attacks its prey.

CLIFF AND EDEN

A stretch of the river, and cliff, the cavern below and the arid plateau at the top of it, and, in the far distance, the girdle of dark and mighty trees which is the boundary of Eden. It is clear that the river is flowing in that direction.

OUTSIDE EDEN

A platoon of Gabriel's soldiers, their arms and their faces shining in the darkness, marches outside the high, dark wall of trees. We realise that the Tigris is flowing below them, deep underground.

We pass through the belt of trees and emerge into the more open spaces of Eden with the earliest light of approaching dawn.

DAWN MIST

The spreading clouds of such mists; how they hang and thicken over a cold stream bed; how they condense into dewdrops along every twig; how the mist becomes suffused with the opalescence of dawn colours; etc. Above all, the moving coils of the mist—the first of many serpentine suggestions which may be noticeable on this fatal morning.

THE FOUNTAIN

It is the basin of a natural spring, wide and very deep. The branch of the Tigris bubbles up here, overflows at one side, and becomes an open stream flowing away between the trees.

Visible a long way down in the clear water, Satan ascends vertically. He steps onto a flat rock at the edge of the basin and sets off through the mist which hangs over the bank of the stream.

THE BOWER

In the earliest light. No bird song. Everything is cold grey, silver, dim green, lavender. We are aware of the grasshopper on the tall grass stem and the dewdrops hanging on the spider web, ready to be fired by the first ray of sunlight.

ADAM

He is asleep. He begins to wake. He flings an arm out over the space beside him as if to embrace Eve. We now see that the space is empty. Adam, much surprised, awakens fully. He raises himself, and looks around, and sees:

EVE

Sitting outside, twenty paces away, with her back to us. She is sitting on a rock or tree trunk, looking out over a little valley.

Adam comes toward her. As he does so he calls to her, slightly disquieted.

>ADAM
>
>Eve!

She doesn't hear him. He steps up to her.

ADAM AND EVE

He puts his hand on her shoulder, and feels it startlingly cold. Eve detaches herself from her brooding stare at stars which have long disappeared. She drags herself over her reluctance to face Adam. She turns her face slowly toward him. She lifts it as if up out of a drowning.

>ADAM
>
>Eve!

EVE

I came out here. For a moment.

ADAM

But you're chilled all through.
The dew hangs in your hair.
Fanciful Eve, you've sat here
half the night, your thoughts
among the stars.

EVE

No. No.

ADAM

Oh, yes. You're shivering.

Eve angrily shakes her head. Adam suspects something.

ADAM

Trembling, then!

Eve starts up and turns away from him, and moves toward the table.

EVE

Why should *I* be afraid?

Adam is following her. He is on the point of making a reply when he notices something. He stands still and turns his head a little, listening intently. Eve stops a pace or two ahead and looks back at him, wondering. He lifts a finger.

ADAM

How quiet the woods are! Nothing
moves! No sound! Some evil has
been here. *Why should you be
frightened?* Did it call to you,
Eve? Did it try to draw you away
from me? Was it that . . . ?

Eve has become more and more apprehensive with every line. To deflect further questions, she takes the offensive:

EVE

Ask first who tried to draw
you away from me.

She turns again and continues to the table, setting out drinking vessels and food. She brings water from the spring that gushes out of the great rock against which the bower is built. The sun is now rising, and the scene begins to flush with colour. Adam comes up to Eve, meaning to ask what she refers to. She anticipates him.

EVE

That other.
That *messenger*.

Her tone echoes, and exaggerates, Satan's quietly contemptuous enunciation of the last word. Adam does not understand her until she points to the seat at the table where Raphael sat the previous evening. Adam is shocked.

ADAM

God's great ambassador?

EVE

Messenger!
I know the names of things.
I know the difference.

ADAM

How can you know, who've never
seen another? What other?

Eve is afraid. She takes her water gourd and crosses to the spring. But as she is filling the gourd, she realises Adam has come up behind her.

ADAM

What other did you speak of?

EVE

Perhaps . . . of God Himself.
You've told me how He talked
with you, when you were here
alone. Gracious, you said—

ADAM

And kind.

EVE

Not so that angel. *He* hurt me.

ADAM

He never touched you.

EVE

By what he said.

ADAM

Nor spoke to you.

EVE

Not once. Nor looked. Nor
smiled. But spoke to you. And
told you not to love me. *Carnal
love! A mere outside,* he said—
that mere messenger! *A creature
incomplete!* Who made me incomplete?
Who finds me incomplete? Do you?

ADAM

Not I.

EVE

Nor yet his better.

ADAM

What . . . ?

EVE

That's how he hurt me.

She bursts into tears. Adam at once forgets his question.

ADAM

Eve!

He puts an arm around her. She sobs.

EVE

He hurt me.

ADAM

His brightness hurt our eyes
when first he came. Because
he came from Heaven. God and
His great angels are not made
to tickle us with pleasures.
But we are made by God, to do His
will, and to obey Him.

> EVE
>
> Or else He hurts us? Don't say
> that God is like that angel—
> proud and cruel and hard.

Adam sets his hand on the wall of rock.

> ADAM
>
> No. But like this rock. See how the
> living water flows from it. See where
> this frail flower blooms on its breast.
> In happiness. But strike your hand
> against it—

He does so.

> ADAM
>
> —and it hurts. If we do
> what is bad . . .

He licks his skinned knuckles.

> EVE
>
> But I don't *want* to do what is
> bad. I want what *I* do to be good.

Baffled, charmed, and amused, Adam throws up his hands, laughs, takes Eve's gourd of water and moves toward the table.

> ADAM
>
> We'll eat, and then to work.

EVE'S FACE

Wearing the look of one who has too much on her mind, and too much on her conscience, to handle. She decides to make the best of it; she chokes down her disturbed feelings and goes to join Adam.

A GLADE AT NOONDAY

An open space a little over a hundred yards in length, and about a third as wide. At one end there is a plot of tillage—mostly melons, squash, gourds, etc., grown on low ridges a few feet apart and covering the intervening ground with their vines. At this end the glade is enclosed by huge cedars.

At the other end of the glade there is no cultivation. Here the enclosing wood is of sweet chestnut trees, very massively and in some cases grotesquely formed in their leaning trunks or enormous branches. Two or three of these trees stand clear of the forest some distance out in the open glade. Between these and the edge of the forest there are spreads of hypericum or asphodel or similar low growth.

ADAM AND EVE

Adam and Eve are at that end of the glade where the cedars grow. The noon meal is over. Adam is stretched on his back, sprawled in the attitude of the farm labourer taking his midday nap.

EVE

She is trying to sleep, and is so nearly asleep that some vestige of her dream is able to rise into her mind.

She opens her eyes and tries to recapture the elusive memory. It is connected in some way with the great cedar trees in the forest behind her. She turns her head that way—perhaps she has avoided looking in that direction all the morning. She looks more and more attentively at the trees. She gets to her feet and slowly crosses to a spot a few paces away. From this point she will see deep into the forest. While she is still crossing toward it:

ADAM

Eve's movement wakes him. He looks up as she passes him.

>ADAM
>Well, are you rested? I am.
>Do you feel better?

>EVE
>Yes.

She speaks tonelessly, continues walking slowly toward the trees.

>ADAM
>The ditch needs cleaning
>out. Look to the ground
>under the trees down there.

Adam points to the other end of the glade.

>EVE
>Yes.

>ADAM
>Those that stand out in the sun
>have dropped their seeds already.

EVE

She is looking intently into the forest.

> ADAM
>
> They'll soon be sprouting if
> we don't clear them up.

> EVE
>
> Clear up the seeds?

She speaks uncertainly, hypnotised by what she sees in the wood.

THE FOREST

As Eve sees it. We are looking at a scene in which the natural features are recognisable as part of the enchanted dream landscape where Eve was first seen walking toward the Tree. The broad black levels of the cedar foliage frame a large datura hung with ghostly white blooms. In the dark recesses of the wood there are spreads of pale and glistening wood lilies.

EVE

Her reaction on seeing this. All the morning she has been trying to keep the dream out of her mind; now it seems to be reality.

Adam comes up to Eve.

> ADAM
>
> We'd better soon begin.

Eve turns a haunted face toward him.

> EVE
>
> Adam . . .

> ADAM
>
> What now?

> EVE
>
> I didn't tell you. I pretended
> it was something else. But . . .
> last night . . . I dreamed again.

> ADAM
>
> Well, then, you dreamed again.
> I know it's not . . .

> EVE
>
> But in my dream I tasted of the Fruit.

Adam is shocked. But Eve looks so pale and distraught that he instinctively protects her. After a pause:

> ADAM
> Don't look so afraid. You
> think of it often enough. What's
> a dream but a loose thought—
> like a wandering star? It slips
> through your mind at night. You
> see it—and it's gone.
>
> EVE
> It's not gone.

She points into the woods.

> EVE
> By daylight it's no different.
> Which is real?

Adam takes her limp hand and strikes it against his chest.

> ADAM
> This. This is real.

Eve is desperately anxious to accept this.

> EVE
> Of course it was a dream. I
> was walking through the wood
> there.
> Lightly, like floating along.
>
> ADAM
> Certainly a dream.

Eve is losing Adam. She begins to talk as if out of a trance. More and more, she is reliving her experience.

> EVE
> Every leaf was like an eye.
> Looking on blessings. Every
> flower's throat had a voice in
> it—praising. And the trees
> were fountains of great voices—
> praising.

ADAM

Praising God.

Distraught as she is, Eve summons up courage enough to pronounce her enormous heresy:

EVE

Praising themselves. Praising
the life in them.

ADAM

What life but in Him?

EVE

The Tree was shining and singing
with life.

ADAM

You ate the Fruit of it?

EVE

Yes.

ADAM

Of course it was a dream. But
still . . .

He becomes still more shocked when he sees that Eve is no longer feeling guilty but rather obscurely excited by the memory of her experience.

She moves her mouth in an attempt to recapture the elusive flavour of the Fruit. Adam watches these movements. Finding himself annoyed, he adopts a superior, puritanical tone.

ADAM

To taste it is to die.
Did you dream you died?

Eve smiles at her recollection of something so different from dying.

EVE

Died?
No.

Eve turns away from Adam. She takes one or two random steps, halts again, and speaks in a voice sometimes loud, sometimes a private mumble.

EVE

I rose up through the air.
Enfolded by . . . the night.
On the breathing breast of . . .
the sky.
Listening to . . . such music.
And I saw the Garden. And all the
living things in it. And living
things outside it.

ADAM

No such things!

EVE

Wild things. Strange things.
Made of the dust of angels
that were . . .

ADAM

Disordered fancy!

EVE

I saw the whole world. Far below.
And all the stars around me. And . . .

ADAM

You rose up all unaided?
To such great height?

EVE

Higher and higher.

ADAM

Alone?

EVE

As if an angel bore me.

ADAM

It was a dream.

EVE

And heard the great suns shouting
with joy on their courses. Their
hair—how it flames and streams!

ADAM

You're dreaming now—by daylight.

Eve's exalted mood vanishes. She hangs her head and mumbles:

EVE

. . . of greatness and beauty
cast down . . .

ADAM

But now—wake up! I'll move
this heavy clay. And you clean up
the ground beneath those trees.

Eve resists. For a moment her memories seem to swallow her up. Her eyes half closed, she speaks with desperate, obstinate conviction:

EVE

I saw star masses, there in middle
space, spout out from one great
womb. Countless worlds being born.

Adam, now tired of all this, and a little uneasy, gives her an affectionate slap on the shoulder. It rouses her. Adam seizes her hand and tugs her to where the tools are lying. He exclaims briskly:

ADAM

There's work to do.

EVE

Sweeping up seeds!

She picks up her rake and wooden shovel. She gives Adam a desolate look and moves away toward the far end of the glade.

ADAM

Troubled by Eve's mood, but soon intent on his work, he takes his clumsy mattock and starts deepening the little irrigation ditch which runs along the side of the patch of melons.

EVE

She comes to one of the trees which stand alone at the end of the clearing. The fallen chestnut burrs are lying scattered on the ground beneath it. Eve leans her shovel against the trunk of the tree and begins to rake the nuts into a heap. A low mound nearby is all that remains of a heap made in some earlier season, and rotted down to almost nothing.

SATAN

We are looking straight at him. His minimum camouflage has hitherto made him invisible to us. He is standing in a thicket at the edge of the forest. He has fixed a ravenous gaze upon Eve.

Eve now has her back to Satan, as she turns to rake more of the seeds toward her. Satan, casual as a dancer and yet precise as a clock, moves toward her, always from behind. He reaches a little twiggy sapling, between five and six feet high, very close to where Eve is working. He conceals himself in this scanty shelter.

EVE AND SATAN

Satan watching Eve. She pities the seeds she is destroying. He pities Eve.

Having raked up a mound of the chestnut burrs, Eve picks up one of them.

EVE AND THE SEED

The burr has split wide open. Inside, the nut itself has split; its halves are spreading into cotyledons; an inch or two of the translucent white root is visible.

Eve cups the living seed in her hand and bends her head to look at it.

EVE AND SATAN

His love for Eve is so great that he may yet be swerved from his purpose.

A shout from Adam a hundred yards away at the far end of the glade.

ADAM

He has straightened up on the edge of his ditch, and is waving his hand to Eve.

EVE AND SATAN

Satan sees Eve drop the sprouted seed onto the heap, and turn in loving response to Adam.

SATAN

His face becomes sad and cruel. He raises an arm to point at Eve as if pronouncing sentence on her. In his jealous eyes she has betrayed the worship of life and change.

SATAN'S ARM

The rest of him is losing substance. All his force and life, and now even his physical being, are flowing into this arm. It writhes and undulates with immense vitality, and soon pours itself on to the ground. It lengthens as it does so. It has become a Serpent.

SATAN THE SERPENT

Its skin is of a milky colour, but overlaid with a shimmering iris. At any moment any of the colours of the iris may deepen or intensify. Thus the Serpent is more colourful and more changeable than a chameleon.

It glides under the asphodel, heading for a point between Eve and the edge of the wood.

EVE

She has resumed her work. Now she is facing the edge of the wood.

EVE AND THE SERPENT

Milky white, with a singularly lustrous black eye, the Serpent raises its head a few inches above the low-growing ground cover. It weaves a little from side to side. Eve looks open-mouthed at the Serpent. It is of a sort she has never seen before. She starts toward it.

The Serpent waits for her, still weaving, beckoning, alluring. When at last she stands close to it, it opens a velvet-lined mouth coloured like the inside of a pomegranate. Darting out a black and forked tongue, it licks the ground at her feet, and it licks her feet.

Eve leans down to touch, to caress, to take hold of this agreeable creature.

It can hardly have disappeared under her hand, and yet, most extraordinarily, it is no longer there.

Eve looks across the spread of asphodel.

THE ASPHODEL

A ripple in the asphodel, a glimpse of milky white, shows Eve that the Serpent is gliding toward the wood.

She follows, already stretching out her hand.

THE SERPENT

It is quite plainly there, just under Eve's hand. She can't possibly miss it. She bends lower, in the very act of touching the Serpent. There is no Serpent there. Eve looks bewildered. She gapes in amazement when she sees:

THE SERPENT

Gliding slowly across a few feet of bare ground, and then into the undergrowth at the edge of the wood. Eve, determined not to let it escape her, follows.

THE WOOD

Eve goes into the wood. She is visible among the trees, in a manner reminiscent of her dream. She is looking around her in all directions. Soon we lose sight of her.

SATAN

After a moment's interval, Satan steps out from the edge of the wood, a little aside from the place where Eve went in. He moves with that sort of unhurried swiftness which is noticeable in a magician at work. He steps straight up to the little sapling behind which he concealed himself while watching Eve. At the far end of the glade, Adam is still delving.

SATAN AND THE SAPLING

A shrub or tree which has leaves of dark green or copper or purple on the top side, and is very pale on the underside.

Satan ripples a hand up and down over this little tree. The leaves obediently turn their dark sides and their pale sides this way and that. The sapling becomes an image of a woman—the dark cascade of her hair, the light on a shoulder and a breast. Impressionistic at six feet; at a hundred yards it would be a completely realistic figure—a maukin—of Eve. Yet there is something a shade obscene about it, and Satan permits himself a sneer as he adds a cynical finishing touch. He looks insolently to where Adam is toiling at the far end of the glade and starts back toward the wood.

EVE IN THE WOODS

Looking on all sides for the Serpent; about to give up the search; obscurely hurt by the Serpent avoiding her. At the last moment she sees it again, its head erect, weaving and beckoning. She hastens toward it.

EVE AND THE SERPENT

The skin of the Serpent, always flushing with new colours, seems to dissolve from its own pattern into the reticulated pattern of sun-spot and leaf-shadow on the forest floor and on the trunks of the trees. This mixture of hot light and hot shade, moving as the leaves move, seems in turn to take on the nature of the twisting, sliding snake. The whole world seems to be made of the slithering Serpent coils. At other moments, the individual Serpent erects itself, gleaming, in the cavern of darkness created by some arched and densely foliaged bough.

We begin to lose our sense of reality and to become one with Eve as she trips and stumbles through the wood, with the trees seeming to sway and the ground rocking under her feet. At last she reels through a thicket.

THE GLADE

Eve has burst out from the comparative darkness of the wood into a hot glare of sunlight. She is in the long narrow glade at the head of which stands the Tree of Knowledge of Good and Evil. Between Eve and the Tree lies less than a hundred feet of lush grass, knee-high, studded with small flowers.

Eve, giddy, and dazzled by the hot light, sees the grasses wave as the Serpent glides toward the Tree. She stumbles after it.

THE SERPENT

Momentarily visible as it leaves the grass and passes over a narrow belt of bare ground which lies around the Tree.

EVE

Eve comes up to the Tree. She takes two of the heavy, downward-curving branches and presses them apart, looking into the clear space under the Tree for the Serpent.

UNDER THE TREE

A clear, deep shade, such as one finds under a weeping mulberry tree—darkness visible. A few flecks of light leak in through the close-packed, glossy foliage. Here and there the young and more translucent leaves on a newly opening spray, or a cluster of the crimson and plum-blue Fruit, may offer something of the effect of a tiny stained-glass window. A chapel for a Black Mass!

In this still, hot and luminous shade, the Serpent, larger, lustrous and enamelled, is to be seen coiled around the trunk of the Tree. His head is extended toward Eve. But even as Eve sees him his form begins to disappear. He says so softly that it is almost like a liquid sound in the music:

SERPENT

Beautiful Eve!

Eve parts the branches wider and lowers her head and steps in under the Tree.

The trunk rises nine or ten feet before dividing. Its thick branches curve upwards and outwards and then down until they touch the ground. The space enclosed is a circle of some sixteen feet in diameter.

Eve has bowed her head in order to pass between the boughs. When she raises it again—

TREE TRUNK AND SERPENT

The Serpent has almost completely disappeared. Now the last traces of him are gone. He seems to have sunk into the Tree. Was his lustrous, enamelled coat only an illusion made by flecks of colored light on the smooth grey trunk of the Tree?

But something is alive under that smooth bark. It seems to flush with gold and bronze colours not its own. It moves with the rippling of muscles. Satan is in the Tree. He *is* the Tree.

The next moment he has stepped clear of the trunk, his arms upraised in the same curve as that of the branches. He lowers them, extends his hands to Eve, and says, in an echo of the words the Serpent uttered to Eve, but in his own, stronger voice:

> SATAN
> Beloved Eve!

Eve is bewildered, giddy with surprise and memories, suffocated by the expansion of her heart.

> EVE
> Are you the Serpent, then?
> You, the great angel, sliding on
> the ground?
>
> SATAN
> The serpent and the angel
> and the tree. Evil and good
> and knowledge.
>
> EVE
> But you, yourself . . . ?
>
> SATAN
> Partake of all, and dwell within
> a tree. Or in a serpent. Eve,
> your children shall one day worship
> trees. And serpents. And stranger
> things.
>
> EVE
> But, of this Tree, the Fruit . . .

Satan plucks a Fruit. He holds it for her to see.

SATAN

Knowledge—of good and evil.
The warp and weft of life.
Each naught without the other.
Will you be naught?

Eve shrinks away from the Fruit as Satan offers it.

EVE

To taste or even touch it is to
die.

SATAN

Taste it—and be a god.

EVE

I fear to die.

SATAN

Then, Eve, fear birth,
the other side of dying. You
saw that—did you not?—
through goddess eyes, when first
you tasted this.

He thrusts the Fruit nearer to her. Eve puts up a hand to keep it away.

EVE

But that was in a dream.

SATAN

Was I *then* a dream? Am I *now* a
dream? What do you know but
dreams? In you, they wail and
sing like winds in a cloven tree.
A fruitless, hollow tree. Cloven
and incomplete! A mere outside!

Eve looks at him, startled and wounded by this echo. Satan adds, casually:

SATAN

Not much to be loved.
But, having tasted this,
knowing all, breathing life
like a god! The goddess,
Eve, whom all the world must
worship. Adam first.

>   As you love him. You love him
>   like a god?
>
> EVE
>
>   But then to die!
>
> SATAN
>
>   How else be born again?

He takes her face in his hands. He looks long and lovingly into her eyes.

> SATAN
>
>   Born into me.

Eve's face takes on the blissful, mindless look of a woman overwhelmed by an infatuation. Satan is now sure he has won. He gently presses Eve to her knees, which in any case are giving way under her. He holds the Fruit in both hands, offering it to Eve, as a priest offers the Host.

> SATAN
>
>   I am Life. Reborn out of
>   good and evil. Knowing both.
>   Beautiful Eve, beloved Eve, eat
>   of me, drink of me.

He holds the Fruit to her lips. Eve looks up at him in desperate, pathetic appeal. She is begging to be spared. But after his next speech she is begging only for the courage to bite, and this his glance will give her.

> SATAN
>
>   And be beautiful and beloved
>   for ever.

Eve opens her mouth to bite.

ADAM

Busy deepening the ditch. He straightens up and waves and smiles at the maukin.

THE MAUKIN

As Adam sees it. It is waving and smiling in a very realistic fashion. Suddenly it becomes a little twiggy sapling again. A terrible cry from Adam.

Adam bounds toward the end of the clearing. His heavy hoe is in his hand.

UNDER THE TREE

Our eyes, newly come from the bright sunlight, see things only dimly for the first few seconds. Eve is in the embrace of a shadowy figure. It is that of Satan, who is in the act of disappearing. His head is bent over hers. Her mouth is greedily biting into the Fruit. Satan's form loses substance. The next moment it has dwindled to nothing.

Eve's arms are clasping the empty air. A small, drably coloured snake slithers down between her breasts, and glides rapidly away.

Eve, her mouth stained with the juice of the Fruit, moves a pace or two, staggering, inflamed by what might equally be an erotic or a religious ecstasy.

FOREST EDGE, GLADE, AND TREE

Adam bursts out of the wood. He sees the trail of crushed grasses left by Eve and the Serpent as they crossed to the Tree.

To the agonising sound of hard-drawn breath and thudding, bursting heart-beat, he rushes across the open space, and up to the Tree.

He parts the boughs as Eve did, and stares inside.

EVE UNDER THE TREE

Hearing, and then seeing, Adam. The tumultuous feelings that possess her suddenly reorientate themselves as swiftly as the shadows swung around when Raphael blazed in the sky. They all project themselves on to Adam. Utterly forgetting Satan, Eve opens her arms to Adam as he pushes the boughs apart and steps toward her. We see that the half-eaten Fruit is still in her left hand.

Adam's eyes are on the Fruit. Eve quickly puts her hand behind her back. Adam grasps her arm roughly. He looks at her stained mouth. He speaks in a hollow, toneless voice.

> ADAM
> You have eaten. You are dead.
> Dead!

> EVE
> *Far* from dead. I burn, I
> throb with life.

She pauses to savour the sensation. Her face flushes; her eyes shine. Careless of her sin, she whispers invitingly:

> EVE
> Adam!

> ADAM
> You heard the angel. Only
> last night. *Eat, and you die!*

Eve talks like one drugged. She looks upward, turning her head from side to side. Adam's words are echoing in her befuddled, guilty mind. Also, her advance has been rejected.

> EVE
>
> *Die? Dead?* I suppose you want me dead. *Die! Die!* you say. *Dead! Dead!* I hear you shouting it all over the sky. Or is it God who shouts it?

A cruel suspicion stabs her.

> EVE
>
> You think He'll give you another Eve, when I'm dust.

> ADAM
>
> When you are dust? You?

> EVE
>
> Like the seeds we rake up, which go to dust. Blown on the wind. Adam, my dust, riding the wind, will weep. If you take another Eve. Such tears! Such rains! They'll drown the world.

> ADAM
>
> I want no other Eve. One has brought ruin enough. After what you heard, last night, with your own ears—what the angel said . . .

> EVE
>
> A greater told me . . . he was here . . . he told me if I ate I should know all of life. I should become a goddess.

She fixes her eyes on Adam as she speaks, imploring him to tell her she has not been deceived. She wipes the juice from her chin with the back of her hand.

> EVE
>
> And you would love me wholly. I loving you as if you were a god.

Even as she speaks she realises she has been cheated in some way. Her eyes fill with tears. Adam looks at her for a long time. He speaks cheerlessly, churlishly.

> ADAM
>
> You've been beguiled by some accursed fraud. And ruined me with you.
>
> EVE
>
> Ruined *you?* No!
>
> ADAM
>
> No! No! You shan't. Oh, God, now look on me! I cast her off.

He swings around and makes an inglorious exit from under the Tree.

EVE

Her euphoric, erotic, intoxicated dream is shattered by the harsh reality: Adam has deserted her. Her cracked and feeble smile lingers from the dream. Under it, a dreadful look of loss and despair begins to surface. Eve crouches, her lips moving in soundless, mindless syllables; idiotic—utterly lost.

Suddenly the boughs are savagely wrenched apart, and Adam bursts in under the Tree as violently as he left it.

Adam is furious with Eve, and terrified of what he is now compelled to do. His voice is harsh, ungracious.

> ADAM
>
> How can I live without you?
> Bone of my bone! Flesh of
> my flesh!
> There's nothing for me now to do
> but die. I don't *want* to die.

He snatches the half-eaten Fruit from Eve's hand. Eve weakly tries to stop him. Adam holds her at arm's length. Fixing his eyes morosely on her:

> ADAM
>
> Nor live, when you are gone.
> So—

He raises his other hand to his mouth and bites into the Fruit.

ADAM

Now—*I* am dead.

As he swallows, his furious, miserable, terrified expression begins to change. He is experiencing a new and thrilling sensation.

SATAN

High above the Earth, he has been looking down, watching Adam. Now he flings up his arms in triumph and utters a cry of exultation.

SATAN'S CRY

It bursts from him like a bomb. It spreads like a ripple through the whole of space. We not only hear it thrilling and throbbing—we can actually see this giant sound wave widening its vast circle. The stars, as it reaches one constellation after another, shudder under its impact like small boats at anchor heaving in a wash.

SUN AND EARTH

Now the stars throw down their spears
And water Heaven with their tears.

Uriel, standing in the sun, throws down his spear, and shoots up vertically toward Heaven. On Earth, seen from the sun, Gabriel's bright troops are rising like rockets from all around the perimeter of Eden.

UNDER THE TREE

Adam exultant. He has been expecting a thunderbolt; none has arrived. Eve is clinging to his arm, looking up at him in adoration. Adam feels like a hero. He can scarcely believe he has survived.

ADAM

Not dead, but much alive!

HIS EYES SHINE

HELL GATE

Lit by the lurid flame from inside. The drawbridge to nowhere, formed by the falling out of the last section of the gate, still projects into the darkness like the apron of a beehive. Like luminous bees, Satan's chief aides are resting on the end of it, or circling lazily in the dark deeps of space. A few lesser spirits have ventured out to join them as they wait for Satan. Sin and Death are seated on either side of the outer part of the gate.

The sound-and-shock wave strikes the spirits flying farthest out, and in the next second has lifted and dropped all the others, and smacked against the rocky dome of Hell. Sin and Death lift their faces and look eagerly outward. All the spirits, great and small, that have been lolling or circling outside now stream in between the sentinels, eager to gain the shelter of Hell. Brittle cries are heard; frightened laughter, high-keyed hysterical triumph. They fear some counterstroke from Heaven.

THE TREE

Seen from outside, and lit by the last fiery red of sunset. The boughs are violently parted. Adam and Eve sally out, each clutching a big cluster of the Fruit. They feel themselves to be lords of the Earth—and so they are. They are also a little arrogant, a little gross, a little absurd. Their faces are flushed and fatuous. Their eyes glitter. Walking on air, they pass from the Tree, along the track through the tall grass, into the forest. Just before they disappear, we see Adam take a Fruit from the cluster Eve is carrying, take a big bite of it, and then carelessly throw the rest away. He flings an arm around Eve. They enter the forest.

SATAN

Flying through space, like an arrow of darkness, as he did in his earlier flight.

HELL GATE

Sin and Death sitting as before. They are peering more eagerly than ever into the deeps of space in the hope of seeing Satan return.

HELL

Seen on all planes and in all its states of existence at the same time. We see spirits—singly, then tens, hundreds, thousands of them—rising from all parts of Hell and converging on Pandemonium.

Wild chattering, nervous laughter, screams of delight, hysterical cries of fear.

PANDEMONIUM

The vociferous spirits crowding thickly in at the door. The last few spirits, desperate and flying fast, come sweeping in from the sulphurous sky of Hell. They dive in through the open doorway.

WITHIN PANDEMONIUM

The whole palace is closely packed with spirits, sitting in a breathless silence, utterly still, wondering which will come first, God's counterstroke or Satan's arrival.

THE BOWER

By late twilight or moonlight. Before we can even recognise the bower, we hear the song. Primitive, wild, romantic, lewd, earthy, animal, utterly careless of consequences—it is the song of profane love which Adam and Eve are singing to each other. The sound of it falters, and ceases.

INSIDE THE BOWER

We dimly see Adam and Eve lost in a ravenous kiss. It is the beginning of a night of orgiastic sensuality.

HELL GATE

A rush of darkness surges up to the apron and condenses into the form of Satan. As he strides up to the gate itself, Sin and Death rise up from their seats. He motions them down, to wait. They sink like barely controllable hounds into their places. Satan passes between them and into Hell.

PORTICO, PANDEMONIUM

Satan lands on the portico. He looks through the door at the packed, silent, crouching figures of his followers. He disappears.

WITHIN PANDEMONIUM

We see part of the close-packed, high-level galleries, and over part of the floor of the main hall, crammed with spirits which seem to have been frozen into immobility, and the next moment we are in the council chamber, where the thousand great seraphic lords are sitting, also frozen, on their thrones.

SATAN'S EMPTY THRONE

Satan's aides are grouped on either side, also immobile as sphinxes. Suddenly a star of the utmost brightness appears on Satan's throne. It grows quickly to Satan's size, and the next moment his form is visible to everyone in the palace. A universal shout of acclaim is silenced when Satan raises his hand. It finds expression only in a seething among the layers upon layers of spirits in the outer hall, which we can see as a momentary transparency imposed on the chamber itself.

SATAN

He shouts:

> SATAN
> I bring you victory.
> Great God has given up His be-
> loved Man, and all His world.
> For Sin and Death to prey on.
> For you to rule.
> As Gods! Gods! Gods!

A silence. And then the burst of applause. It goes on and on.

THE TRANSFORMATION

Moloch is applauding furiously. His complexion begins to darken. His face takes on the contours of the iron idol of Tophet and Carthage. Smoke ascends. His empty eyes glare yellow with the light of flames within him.

Looking from side to side, we witness other changes. Satan's aides are taking on the forms that we associate with their deification in Egypt or Asia Minor. Others become the idols of remoter regions and more fantastic faiths. We see many serpent gods—Norse, Teutonic, Chinese, Aztec, etc. Other angels, with raised arms and spreading hair, are in rapid metamorphosis into sacred trees. We see the many-armed and the elephant-headed gods of India, the staring feather masks from the South Seas, the crocodile-headed fetish from the Ivory Coast. Inca gods, Mayan gods, dragons, standing stones—every conceivable deity, demon or monster that has ever been worshipped by men.

Moreover, the lower-ranking angels are at the same time transformed into imps, trolls, incubi, succubi, hobgoblins and every gargoyle and reptilian form that has been thought to populate the nether regions or unhallowed spots on Earth.

THE MULTITUDINOUS AND SEETHING TRANSFORMATION AS A WHOLE

Among these devilish forms some are lighter in colour and some darker than the rest. By an obscure affinity, numbers of the darker sort congregate in inky blots or shadowy streaks in certain areas, while the lighter ones, streaming through the close-packed mass, trace curving lines or set points of highlight here and there. A pattern is forming and dissolving and forming again; we are watching the emergence of forms already vaguely familiar to us, and which at any moment will become recognisable.

This effect persists and increases, not only in the general view of the transformation, but while we are watching the swarming flight that follows.

SATAN

Surprised at first, he soon grasps the principle behind the transformation of the fallen angels into monstrosities. He himself undergoes no change except for that implicit in the devilish irony with which he regards the degeneration of those who are, in one aspect, extensions of himself. He shouts derisively:

> SATAN
>
> See! Now you are yourselves!
> Up then! The Earth awaits you.
> Enter, now, into your godlike bliss!
> Gods! Gods! Gods!

PORTICO OF PANDEMONIUM

Satan standing in the doorway. All the others pouring out past him; he urging them on like a huntsman unkennelling the hounds.

> SATAN
>
> Devils! Demons! Fiends!

He disappears.

HELL GATE

Satan in the middle of the gate. Sin and Death watching him, tense, slavering to be off.

> SATAN
>
> Sin! Death! The world is yours!
> Off, then—and lead the pack.

Sin and Death rush out, ahead of the oncoming mob of false gods and demons, and the whole innumerable company launches itself out like a wide, curving comet-tail.

ADAM AND EVE

They are lying asleep. The pallor of their limbs and clouds of hair and of shadow are reminiscent of the patterns of light and dark which we have observed on the surface of the swarm of demons. After their night of orgiastic love, Adam and Eve sleep deeply but uneasily.

> *and grosser sleep*
> *Bred of unkindly fumes, with conscious dreams*
> *Encumbered . . .*

The dreams which encumber the sleep of Adam and Eve, now that they have the knowledge of good and evil, are confused visions of what is happening in the nether world that very night. Thus from their first guilt springs mankind's first nightmare of wrathful gods and tormenting demons.

As the image of their embraced bodies appeared on the surface of the demon swarm, now the contorted faces of the devils manifest themselves in the light and shade on the flesh of the dreamers. One appalling mask actually thrusts itself out between Eve's shoulder blades.

THE SWARM OF DEMONS

Sweeping through space. Close to us, certain individual monsters are recognisable as those we have seen afflicting the sleep of Adam and Eve.

ADAM AND EVE

The first light of dawn is seeping in. Adam and Eve lie in disordered postures, as if they had been pole-axed. Adam's face is contorted. His arm is flung out. A convulsive twitch brings his fingers into contact with Eve's upper arm. He clutches it as if he were drowning. He comes up into consciousness. At the same moment, his desperate clutch has awakened Eve.

> ADAM
>
> I had the most terrible . . .

Turning their ravaged faces toward each other, both see the reflection of their own.

> ADAM
>
> You too? You dreamed . . . ?
>
> EVE
>
> Of monsters. And of . . .

ADAM

> Again! That other dream!
> Which makes you lick your lips
> while still you taste the bitter-
> ness of death. You dreamt you
> ate . . .

Eve bows her head.

ADAM

> I too! I ate the Fruit.

He tries to deny it.

ADAM

> I *dreamt* I did. You told me of
> *your* dream, and set my thoughts
> turning that way, so that in
> my sleep . . .

As he speaks he looks away from Eve. He hangs his head; his eyes shift uneasily from side to side, out of the way of the truth. But over the last line his voice fades; his jaw drops; he grips Eve's arm again, and points.

FLOOR NEAR COUCH

Lying there is a twig a few inches long, with a couple of glossy leaves on it, and a half-eaten Fruit. It is discoloured and half rotten.

ADAM AND EVE

Raising themselves to look at the Fruit; one crouching, the other on one knee. Everything now comes back to them. They look at each other in deathly silence. Self-loathing, loathing for each other, and above all a dreadful and ever-increasing fear. The tension between them mounts beyond endurance. With a moan, or a desolate cry, each recoils from the other. They are so exhausted and so crushed by their terror that they can scarcely stand upright, yet their mutual repulsion is so violent that they get to their feet simultaneously, and stumble cowering away from each other.

OUTSIDE THE BOWER

Adam and Eve burst out; one from the front and one from the side. Eve runs toward the place where Adam found her sitting the previous morning. Adam rushes toward a stand of tall trees. He blindly collides—we hear the impact—with one of the bare trunks. He clutches at it. He presses his grazed face against the rough bark—guilt seeking pain.

DEEP SPACE

The hornet swarm of demons, with Satan in their midst, and Death and Sin as outriders leading the way.

ADAM

Frantic despair has now given place to an abysmal depression. He is now crouching at the foot of the tree, his head in his hands.

Eve creeps timidly up to him. She touches him. He turns a haggard face toward her. The sight of her speechless wretchedness moves him to a speechless tenderness. He puts his hand to her tear-stained cheek; draws his trembling fingers along the line of her jaw. Her eyes, drained of tears, piteously importune him. His look tries to tell her that he still loves her; but what a look for a lover! Nothing could be more painful, pathetic, or absurd than these woebegone, silent exchanges. They would like to kiss each other. They have not the blood or strength or warmth to move their heads to a meeting. So these pitiful, half-formed kisses die miserably in the void. Adam tries to speak. He wants to utter words of love. He labours with this immense, impotent longing. When at last he is able to speak, the mountain of emotion gives birth to a spiteful little mouse.

> ADAM
> I begged you—Stay beside me.

Eve's submission and remorse at once give place to indignation.

> EVE
> You told me—you *commanded* me
> to go. Go, you said. Sweep up
> the seeds.

> ADAM
> If I said Go, I said it trusting
> you.

> EVE
> A hundred paces off you trusted me!

> ADAM
> And that short way too far. I
> should have kept you close to
> my side.

> EVE
> Close *in* your side, you mean—
> a lifeless rib.

Adam claws at his breast.

> ADAM
>
> Was I not better then, when you
> were locked here, harmless?
>
> A VOICE
>
> Adam!

It is the strong, stern voice of God. It seems to come from the air over the clearing, at a moderate distance above the ground.

Adam and Eve, electrified, dive for cover into a group of young wild fig trees—yearling shoots five or six feet high, rising close together from the ground.

> VOICE OF GOD
>
> Where are you, Adam? You who
> always come with joy to meet Me.
> Why try to hide?
> I see you now, as I have always
> seen you.
> And saw you yesterday.
> Come out!

Adam and Eve reluctantly come out of the fig tree growth. They have broken off one or two branches, and hold them across their middles in some sort of sketchy gesture toward covering themselves. Adam looks up and in all directions, but sees nothing.

> ADAM
>
> Lord God, I cannot see You.
>
> VOICE OF GOD
>
> Nor shall you, Adam, while you live
> on Earth. You have eaten of the
> Fruit that I forbade. In doing that,
> you lost the sight of God.
>
> ADAM
>
> You knew that I would do it.
> You, who made me, and made the Fruit,
> made her from whom I took it. Be-
> cause You made her good, and dear to
> me, I took it from her hand.
> And then . . . I ate.

VOICE OF GOD

Woman, what is this thing that
you have done?

EVE

The Serpent told me it would give
me life. I longed for life; therefore I ate the Fruit.

VOICE OF GOD

Poor creature, have a little of
your wish. Have life, and give life,
Eve. But giving it you shall
bring forth in sorrow. Adam, the Earth,
from which I took you, is by your
deed accursed. You shall labor and sweat
upon it. Reap thorns and thistles, till
you go again down to that dead clay from
which you came.

ADAM

Oh, no, Lord, no! Not I! Not I!

VOICE OF GOD

To dust you shall return.

ADAM

No! No! No! No!

VOICE OF GOD

Await My archangel, Michael. He
shall give you safe-conduct from
the Garden. You shall not at once
be slain by all the evils you have
brought from Hell.

Adam sinks his head in his hands. There is a long silence.

THE EMPTY CLEARING

The long silence is broken by the sound of Adam sobbing.

ADAM AND EVE

First Eve, looking to Adam as he crouches beside her; then Adam himself, his head down almost to the ground; his shoulders racked by his misery.

Eve looks at him in infinite compassion. Suddenly she springs up, mad, like a mother who sees her child being tortured.

EVE

She rushes wildly into the clearing, and gestures in frenzy to the air. Eve does not realise, but we soon do, that the air is now empty. Her screams are incoherent; the words sometimes indistinct.

> EVE
> God! Lord! See how he suffers!
> Oh, God, spare him! What did he
> do? *I* gave him the Fruit. He ate
> it to die with me. Oh, God, let him
> live . . . let him live! Let me die
> twice over. Let me suffer for him.
> I was to blame. Only I. I wanted to
> be a goddess. Punish me for both of
> us. Kill me! Send me down to suffer!
> Spare him. Only spare him.

She waits a second or so for a response. She realises there is nothing but the empty air. Clutching her dishevelled hair, her face discoloured, miserably blotched with tear stains, she reaches the depths of despair.

> EVE
> He's not there!
> There's nothing! No one!
> No one! No one! No one!

She spins around, ready to smash herself to the ground in her frenzy. But Adam has come up behind her. He catches her in his arms as she falls.

ADAM AND EVE

> ADAM
> No one but us.

They clutch each other so closely that they seem to become one. Eve buries her face in Adam's breast. Adam seems to have found a new and rather grim sort of strength and protectiveness. Eve lifts her face—troubled, loving, hopeful.

THE UPPER AIR

High above the world, the vast swarm of evil spirits comes wheeling in. Satan, who has been leading, draws aside and signals to the rest to swing past him and into a landing spiral. Sin and Death lead them in this manoeuvre.

ADAM AND EVE

The place where they are still standing is not far from one end of the bower. A slab protrudes from the rock-face outside and forms something like a bench. It is here Adam fashions his tools.

Adam now loosens his embrace.

> ADAM
>
> We've little time.

He crosses to the bench, followed by Eve.

AT ADAM'S WORKBENCH

Hand axes and points of early paleolithic type; two or three wooden hafts, split at one end; strips of palm fibre or other binding material. Scattered chips and half-completed tools are on the bench, and mattocks and picks recently in use are leaning or hanging at the end of the bower.

Adam takes down a mattock and cuts the binding with a sharp-edged flake. As he talks he turns the flat stone blade in the cleft so that its edge is parallel to the haft, thus transforming the harmless mattock into an axe. He soon begins to bind the blade into its new position. He works steadily through the whole of the scene. All speeches are uttered in the most matter-of-fact manner imaginable.

> ADAM
>
> Out there, you saw the lion
> kill the deer.

> EVE
>
> *Passing life on,* he said.

> ADAM
>
> Who kills most, lives most, then.

He hands her a stone point.

> ADAM
>
> Here—you take this. I'll
> haft it for you later.

> EVE
>
> Who loves most lives most, Adam.

> ADAM
>
> Nonetheless, take this.

                    EVE

                    If I must.

She takes it.

                    ADAM

                    Must! That's the word now.
                    And first of many musts—we
                    two must live.

                    EVE

                    Live—yes. But how, out there?

                    ADAM

                    Together, wife. That's how.

                    EVE

                    In gladness, then!

                    ADAM

                    And sorrow.
                    Come better, or come worse . . .

                    EVE

                    Together!

                    ADAM

                    Till death us do . . .

A blinding flash of light interrupts him. When it is gone, they wheel around to see its source.

THE WOODS

The Archangel Michael comes striding through the trees. He has not reduced his size. He is about forty feet high, and the greatest warrior among all the archangels. He holds the Sword of God. Now and then he holds it high in the air and motionless, so that Adam and Eve can see it. At other times he whirls it above his head, or sweeps it rapidly from side to side. At such moments it looks as it did when it guarded the gate—like an electric arc of immensely high voltage.

ADAM, EVE AND MICHAEL

Michael's face is stern. He advances on Adam and Eve and motions them to be on their way. They quickly turn and hurriedly march ahead of him.

He shepherds them into the wood, pointing the Sword down toward them, and using it as a farm hand might use a cattle prod to drive two small animals through a gate.

GATE OF EDEN

Michael steps ahead of Adam and Eve and stands at one side of the gate. Motioning with the Sword, he urges them to pass him and to go into the barren lands outside.

ADAM AND EVE

Holding each other. Stealing a fearful glance at Michael's stern face as they stumble past, their heads at about the level of his knees.

ADAM AND EVE

As soon as they have passed through the gate, their appearance changes. Their features become coarser, their brows heavier, their gait clumsier. They have become specimens of the first *Homo sapiens.* Love in their hearts and weapons in their hands, they shamble out into the hostile world.

MICHAEL

As Adam and Eve pass him, he looks after them. His face is no longer stern. He enters into his second role, as a Guardian Angel. He watches his charges with a hint of a kindly smile.

ADAM AND EVE

As soon as they are completely clear of the gate, Michael disappears. We now see that they are passing the lower legs of another giant figure. The feet are planted in the stamped-out wreckage of Gabriel's pavilion.

SATAN

Looking down at Adam and Eve as they go unseeingly past him. He also smiles—the most enigmatic smile imaginable. As Adam and Eve pass on, Satan raises his eyes and . . .

SATAN

. . . he directs this extraordinary smile straight at us. On Satan's smile, seen closer and closer, his eyes boring into ours, we reach:

THE END